IMAGES
of America

US MILITARY
IN HAWAII
BEFORE 1941

IMAGES
of America

US MILITARY
IN HAWAII
BEFORE 1941

Sarah Bellian

ARCADIA
PUBLISHING

Copyright © 2024 by Sarah Bellian
ISBN 9781-4671-6198-5

Published by Arcadia Publishing
Charleston, South Carolina

Printed in the United States of America

Library of Congress Control Number: 2024938207

For all general information, please contact Arcadia Publishing:
Telephone 843-853-2070
Fax 843-853-0044
E-mail sales@arcadiapublishing.com

Visit us on the Internet at www.arcadiapublishing.com

CONTENTS

ACKNOWLEDGMENTS

Thank you to my volunteers at the Pacific Fleet Submarine Museum, my colleagues at USS *Missouri* (BB-63) and the Pearl Harbor Aviation Museum; Sadie, my historic beach scout; and Kyndal, my favorite ship nerd.

Also, thanks to Meaghann, Kari, Robin, Shekinah, and my other degenerate friends who've served this project as providers of moral support and beer. Sailors have staggered down the streets of Honolulu's Chinatown for the past 200 years. What better way to honor their legacy than to get one more drink at Smitty's?

Images for this book come from the Hawaii State Archives, Navy History and Heritage Command, Battleship Missouri, the Pearl Harbor Aviation Museum, the Tropic Lightning Museum, the Army Museum of Hawaii, and the University of Hawaii's Honolulu Advertiser Collection (Hawaii War Records Depository). There are also many excellent images at the Bishop Museum, the National World War II Museum, the Arizona Memory Project, Magnum Photos, and TIME-LIFE/Getty.

I am particularly grateful for the wonderful archivists at the Hawaiian Historical Society and Peter T. Young of the blog *Images of Old Hawaii*. I also owe a debt to Tai Sing Loo, whose work was the real genesis of this book.

Courtesy Lines:

PFSM	Pacific Fleet Submarine Museum at Pearl Harbor
NHHC	Navy History and Heritage Command
HSA	Hawaii State Archives
HHS	Hawaiian Historical Society
USAMH	US Army Museum of Hawaii (Fort DeRussy)
HWRD	Hawaii War Records Depository, University Archives & Manuscripts Department, University of Hawaii at Manoa Library

INTRODUCTION

The Hawaiian island chain sits in the middle of the Pacific, about 2,400 miles southwest of the California coast and 3,900 miles from Japan. The island of Oahu is where the largest and most populous city, Honolulu, is located. At roughly 604 square miles in size, this small island owes its preeminence to two harbors along its southern shore: Honolulu and Pearl Harbor.

The US Pacific Squadron was established in 1821 as a small force protecting commercial interests. During the Mexican-American War of 1846–1848, it contributed to the capture of what is now California. The United States stretched from "sea to shining sea" and began to look farther.

The uneasy relationship between the United States and Japan can be traced back to 1853, when Commodore Perry's "gunboat diplomacy" forcibly opened the country to the world. By the end of the Spanish-American War, the United States controlled Guam and the Philippines. Hawaii was seen as a vital link between the mainland and these distant territorial possessions. It was also increasingly viewed as an outpost from which to watch, and potentially fight, Japan. Japan remained wary of the intentions of the United States, sending a warship to protest the annexation of Hawaii in 1898. Thousands of Japanese were already working on plantations in Hawaii, and the United States had a blatantly anti-Asian immigration policy.

Although propaganda painted the attack on Pearl Harbor as treachery, it was not unanticipated.

Admirals and generals had rehearsed it in fleet maneuvers for decades. War between the United States and Japan seemed probable 15 years before it began. Soldiers and sailors on Oahu spent the entirety of 1940 training for Japanese attack. There was a good reason Lt. Comdr. Logan Ramsey began his message at 7:58 a.m. on December 7, 1941, with the words "Air raid, Pearl Harbor. This is not a drill."

This is not where the story starts. More than a hundred years before "the day of infamy," the United States military occupation of Hawaii began with the Western world's discovery of what was at the time called "Wai Momi," the beautiful—and unfortunately, strategically located—waters of pearl.

One

THE PEARL OF THE PACIFIC

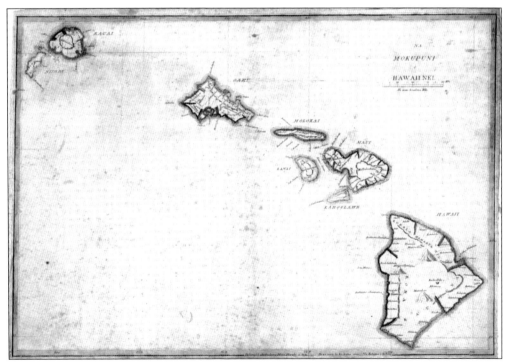

NA MOKUPUNI O HAWAII NEI BY SIMONA P. KALAMA, **1837.** British explorer Capt. James Cook was the first European to reach Hawaii in 1778. When Cook anchored, he was showered with gifts and received in royal fashion. However, after a rowboat was stolen, Cook took a chief hostage and arrogantly tried to exchange him for the boat. Enraged, the Hawaiians killed Cook. (Library of Congress.)

JOHN LEDYARD, C. 1783. One member of Cook's crew was an American, John Ledyard. While their captain was otherwise occupied, Ledyard and his shipmates found women willing to entertain them and attempted an unsuccessful ascent of Mauna Loa with nothing but their blankets and a bottle of brandy. Ledyard's best-selling account of his voyage with Cook was the first US manuscript to receive a copyright. (New Hampshire Historical Society, 1995.588.07.)

FROM "LIFE ON THE OCEAN," GEORGE LITTLE, 1851. Hawaiians were expert navigators. Reefs and shallow water, which posed difficulties for Western ships, were easily accessed by outriggers. Hawaiian double-hulled canoes also successfully crossed vast stretches of the Pacific. This image shows the ship *Dromo* visited by King Tamaamaooa with six war canoes in February 1809. (NHHC 85334.)

KAMEHAMEHA I BY JAMES GAY SAWKINS, 1850. Kamehameha was among those who witnessed Cook's arrival. Impressed with the British ships and weapons, he recognized that whatever he could learn about them would make him powerful. With the goal of uniting the Hawaiian islands, Kamehameha began amassing an army. This portrait of Kamehameha I wearing the 'ahu 'ula (feather cloak of Hawaiian royalty) hangs in Iolani Palace today. (HSA, PP-97-5-007.)

"**TEREOBOO (KALANI'OPU'U), KING OF OWYHEE (HAWAII), BRINGING PRESENTS TO CAPTAIN COOK**" BY JOHN WEBER, 1784. At the time of European contact, there were 300,000 to 800,000 people living on the five major Hawaiian islands. The islands held numerous desirable resources, including humpback whales (oil), pearls, and sandalwood. Numerous bloody confrontations occurred over access to these resources, both between foreigners and Hawaiians and between rival chiefs. (HSA, PP-4-9-009.)

BARBER'S POINT, 2024. In 1796, British captain Henry Barber cheated Kamehameha in a rum deal. He escaped punishment but wrecked his ship *Arthur* off Kalaeloa (Long Cape), now called Barber's Point. Kamehameha's divers salvaged *Arthur*'s guns. The king refused to return the guns when Barber demanded them back and also made Barber pay for his reprovisioning with gunpowder. The lighthouse was established in 1888. (Photograph by Sarah Hausman.)

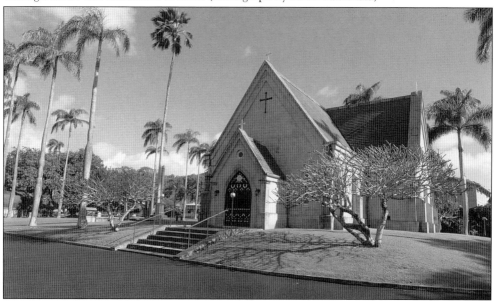

MAUNA ALA, THE ROYAL MAUSOLEUM OF HAWAII, 2024. John Young, an important advisor to Kamehameha I, did not initially intend to stay in Hawaii. While he was ashore investigating the disappearance of the ship *Fair American*, his captain left without him. Young assisted Kamehameha with shipbuilding and foreign affairs and served as governor of Oahu. He married into Kamehameha's family and is buried in the Royal Mausoleum. (Author's photograph.)

KAʻAHUMANU BY ALEXANDER ADAMS, 1817. Many foreign sailors found opportunities with the Kingdom of Hawaii. American Alexander Adams commanded the first Hawaiian-flagged western vessel, *Kaʻahumanu*. In 1817, *Kaʻahumanu* traveled to China to sell sandalwood but paid over $3,000 in port charges, making the voyage too expensive to be profitable. Kamehameha decided that Hawaii should also levy port charges, a move which worried merchants. (HSA, PP-23-2-022.)

COLUMBIA BY GEORGE DAVIDSON, 1793. Following the American Revolution, the new United States was bankrupt. A group of businessmen underwrote a voyage for *Columbia Redivida* under the command of John Kendrick to initiate trade with China. In Hawaii, Kendrick took on sandalwood, which the Chinese had an insatiable desire for. He also observed "a fine deep bay running well to the northward." This bay was Pearl Harbor. (Oregon Historical Society.)

MARKER FOR JOHN KENDRICK AT WALKER PARK, 2024. The first US flag over Pearl Harbor was flown by John Kendrick on his ship, celebrating Kamehameha's victory over Kauai. When a salute was rendered, a gun malfunctioned and killed Kendrick. A replica of his ship *Lady Washington* sails today from Grays Harbor Historic Seaport in Washington. (Author's photograph.)

LITHOGRAPH OF KA'IANA DURING HIS VISIT TO CHINA, 1789. Ka'iana, an *ali'i* (noble) of Puna, Hawaii, would oppose Kamehameha in his conquest of Oahu and lose his life at the Battle of Nu'uanu. He sailed with John Meares on the British vessel *Iphigenia* in 1788 to China, the Philippines, and the Pacific Northwest, where Meares searched for evidence of the fabled Northwest Passage. A courageous Hawaiian woman referred to as Winee (likely "wahine," the Hawaiian word for "woman") also participated in this voyage, She fell ill and died at sea. (British Museum)

14

EARLY ROAD LEADING OVER THE PALI, C. 1898. By 1795, Kamehameha I had assembled the largest army Hawaii had ever seen: 12,000 men and 1,200 war canoes with muskets and cannons. At the Battle of Nu'uanu (May 1795), Kamehameha's forces pushed their enemies over the edge of the Pali (cliff). This battle established Kamehameha I as ruler of Hawaii. When a road was built over the Pali in 1898, workers discovered hundreds of skulls, believed to be the men who fell to their deaths. This site features prominently in local ghost stories. (HSA, PPWD-12-6-011)

NU'UANU STREAM AT HONOLULU HARBOR BY LOUIS CHORIS, 1816. Around 1810, Kamehameha moved his seat of government to Waikiki on Oahu. Honolulu became the favorite port of call for foreigners because of the stability created by Kamehameha. Merchant voyages from the United States to China (and in the 1850s, Japan) needed to resupply coal or water, and Hawaii was positioned perfectly to meet this need. (HSA, PP-37-14-003.)

FORT KEKUANOHU, 1816. In 1815, Kamehameha gave Russians permission to build a storehouse, but instead, they built a fort at what is now Fort and Queen Streets. When Kamehameha saw what was happening, he sent men to remove the Russians—by force if necessary. The Russians wisely decided not to further test the king. Kamehameha named the fort Kekuanohu (thorny scorpion fish), appropriate because it was bristling with guns. (HSA, PP-36-5-002.)

GEORGE KAUMUALI'I TAMOREE BY SAMUEL MORSE, 1816. While the Western world was "discovering" Hawaii, Hawaiians also ventured out themselves. In 1804, Prince George Kaumuali'i Tamoree or "Humehume" was sent to America for school. He instead enlisted in the US Marine Corps and was assigned to USS *Wasp* (1814) during the War of 1812. He also served in the US Navy aboard USS *Enterprise* (1799) during the Second Barbary War. (HHS.)

Two

WHALERS, MISSIONARIES, AND MARTIAL LAW

KA'AHUMANU, CONSORT OF KAMEHAMEHA I, BY LOUIS CHORIS, C. 1832. Missionaries began arriving in Hawaii around 1820. Many of them were appalled by how Hawaiians "lolled about, swam, and surfed" instead of doing what they viewed as "productive work." When one missionary attempted to convert Kamehameha to Christianity, the king told him to throw himself over the Pali, and if he survived, he'd consider it. (HSA, PP-96-6-003.)

TAMEHAMEHA 2?
HIS MAJESTY THE KING OF THE

LIHOLIHO AND QUEEN KAMĀMALU, c. 1824. Kamehameha I died on May 18, 1819, and was succeeded by Liholiho (Kamehameha II). Because Liholiho was not a warrior, he went to Europe in 1823 with the goal of placing Hawaii under the protection of Great Britain. The Hawaiian royals were not received by the king. Instead, the British press mercilessly mocked them, commenting on how fat and dark they were and how the women smoked cigars and played cards. Newspapers decried the "quackery" of "treating these people as European monarchs." While in England, Liholiho and his wife contracted measles, a disease to which they had no immunity. They both deteriorated quickly and died. Their remaining entourage was presented to George IV, a small conciliatory gesture in the aftermath of a tremendous insult and tragic loss. (Both, British Museum.)

"HULA HULA DANCERS," C. 1890.
Powerful Hawaiian women saw certain *kapu* (traditional laws) as barriers to their inclusion and success and were attracted to Christianity as an alternative. One early convert, Queen Ka'ahumanu, sought to liberate Hawaiian women, not realizing that the missionaries were intent on eradicating Hawaiian culture, beginning with the prohibition of songs and dances. (HHS.)

HIRAM BINGHAM BY SAMUEL MORSE, C. 1852. Hiram Bingham led the first group of American Protestant missionaries in Hawaii. After Queen Ka'ahumanu converted to Christianity, she took a strong stance against prostitution and drunkenness. Bingham helped develop a system for writing the Hawaiian language and translated parts of the Bible into Hawaiian. However, the missionary board grew worried about his interference in politics and recalled him in 1840. ("Portraits of American Protestant Missionaries to Hawaii," 1902, University of California.)

SURF SWIMMING, HAWAII.

HAWAIIAN WOMEN SWIMMING, 1888. The sight of women swimming naked in the surf shocked missionaries, but others found traditional island life appealing. One of Hawaii's earliest tourists, Mark Twain wrote, "I observed a bevy of nude native young ladies bathing in the sea, and sat down on their clothes to keep them from being stolen." Twain loved Hawaii and regretted never being able to return. (University of Toronto.)

VIEW of the ISLAND of WOAHOO in the PACIFIC as VISITED by C.E. BENSELL in 1821.

"VIEW OF THE ISLAND OF WOAHOO (OAHU) IN THE PACIFIC" BY C.E. BENSELL, 1821. The first US Navy ship in Hawaii, USS *Dolphin* (1821), arrived on January 16, 1826. Commanding officer "Mad Jack" Percival had been sent to arrest mutineers and collect debts. His crew was furious to learn that they could not buy alcohol and women were forbidden from swimming to their ship. (Peabody Essex Museum, Salem MS, M6437.)

20

CAPT. JOHN PERCIVAL BY BLACK, C. 1861 (RIGHT), AND THOMAS AP CATESBY JONES, C. 1842 (BELOW). "Mad Jack" Percival cursed the missionaries as "a set of damned schoolmasters" and demanded an audience with the queen. The queen replied that she was enforcing Christian behavior. In response, "Mad Jack" declared that if the leader of the missionaries appeared, he would shoot him. A group of drunk sailors began smashing windows, repeating their demands for women. Chaos ensued as merchant sailors joined the Navy. Rioters broke into the home of Hiram Bingham, whose bodyguards clubbed the ringleaders unconscious. The Navy was forced to send a more diplomatic envoy, Capt. Thomas ap Catesby Jones, who arrested the worst offenders. His willingness to "take out the trash" improved feelings toward the US military presence in Hawaii. (Left, US Naval Institute; below, NHHC 1311.)

PEACOCK FIRING SHOTS, APRIL 1814. The ship USS *Peacock* (1813) brought Jones to Hawaii and went on to participate in the 1838 US Exploring Expedition. The expedition gathered information for "the international scientific and intellectual community" (meaning Europe). Thousands of plants and animals unknown to Western science were collected. Indigenous peoples of the Pacific and northwestern North America were also studied, sometimes resulting in explosive confrontations. (NHHC 902975.)

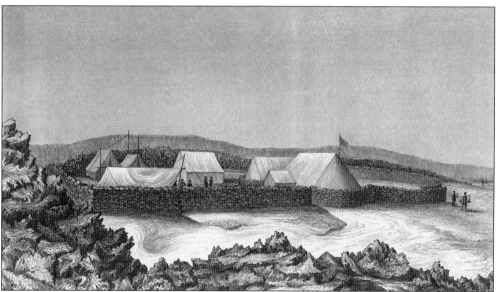

THE US EXPLORING EXPEDITION, 1845. The only physical evidence of the US Exploring Expedition lies near the summit of Mauna Kea volcano. For three weeks in December 1840, a group of scientists and Lt. Charles Wilkes made camp there and conducted experiments in freezing temperatures. Unfortunately, Wilkes was court-marshalled for abusing his men, and the work he oversaw was disregarded. (*Narrative of the United States Exploring Expedition*, Volume IV, 1845, Smithsonian.)

HERMAN MELVILLE, C. 1885 (RIGHT), AND WHALING SHIPS (BELOW). From the 1700s through the mid-1800s, whale oil was used for lighting throughout most of the Western world. Whaling peaked in 1846—at this time, it was the fifth-largest industry in the United States. By the Civil War, whale oil had been replaced by kerosene, and whales had become scarce. Before he became famous for his story of the white whale *Moby Dick*, Herman Melville enlisted on board *United States* at Honolulu in 1843. On his first morning aboard, he witnessed two men receive lashes for fighting and smuggling liquor. Some captains simply abandoned troublesome members of their crew in Hawaii, leaving them to local officials or the US Navy to sort out. (Right, HHS; below, New York Public Library.)

THE PAULET AFFAIR, 1843. On February 10, 1843, British captain Lord George Paulet got into a fight with American businessman Sanford Dole and demanded an audience with Kamehameha III. The king refused. Paulet invaded the palace and lowered the Hawaiian flag. The US Navy issued an ultimatum. If the British did not disavow Paulet's acts, they would "make a fuss." USS *Constellation* (1797), returning from China, saw the British flag flying and flew the Hawaiian flag in response. The American captains of USS *Constellation* and USS *United States* (1797) hosted parties for Hawaiian royalty. Paulet was removed by a British admiral, and by July 31, the Hawaiian flag flew over the palace again. USS *Constellation* (1854) is a museum ship in Baltimore today. It was originally touted as a rebuilt version of the 1797 vessel, but research in the 1990s disproved this. (Both, Library of Congress.)

Three

COMMODORE PERRY AND
THE OPENING OF JAPAN

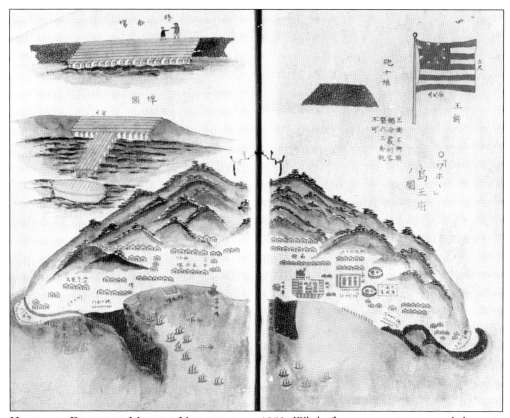

HONOLULU DRAWN BY MANJIRO NAKAHAMA, C. 1850. While flags were going up and down in Hawaii, the US also had its eyes on a more distant prize. Japan had been closed to foreigners since 1603, and anyone who left could not return. Landing sites on Oahu and Maui suggest that before their nation's isolation began, Japanese sailors had already visited Hawaii 500 years before Captain Cook. (HSA, PP-38-1-014.)

MANJIRO NAKAHAMA, C. 1880. In 1853, the *Polynesian Herald* published, "Having visited a foreign country . . . [the Japanese] are not welcomed at home as the unfortunate should be, but are thrust out to become homeless." In 1841, five shipwrecked Japanese fishermen were brought to Honolulu. Manjiro, only 14 years old, traveled to the US mainland and became the first Japanese to live there, learning English and even participating in the 1849 Gold Rush. (Rosenbach Museum & Library.)

MANJIRO'S DRAWING OF JOHN HOWLAND, THE WHALING SHIP THAT SAVED HIM, C. 1850. Manjiro eventually succeeded in returning to Japan, where he was interrogated and ordered to stay away from the sea. When the Japanese government realized he could teach officials English, he was made a samurai and given the surname Nakahama. Men like Manjiro were essential to Japan's astoundingly quick transformation from a feudal society into an industrial one. (Rosenbach Museum & Library.)

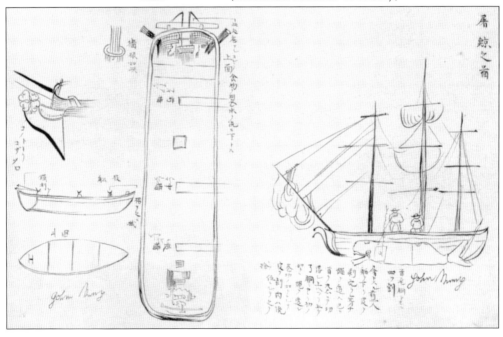

A Japanese Drawing of One of Perry's "Black Ships," c. 1854. The Japanese had never seen anything like the coal-burning American warships, surrounded by clouds of black smoke. They depicted them in art with a striking resemblance to *yokai* (traditional Japanese demons). Note the side-wheel configuration and compare this image to the photograph of the actual USS *Mississippi* (1841) below. (Ryosenji Treasure Museum.)

USS *Mississippi* (1853). The first USS *Mississippi*, a side-wheel steamer, was built under the personal supervision of Commodore Matthew C. Perry and commissioned on December 22, 1841. *Mississippi* took part in experiments crucial to development of the steam Navy and was the flagship of Perry's squadron entering Tokyo Bay on July 8, 1853. She was lost in the Civil War. "Napha (Naha, Okinawa) from the Sea," a c. 1853–1854 lithograph, depicts USS *Mississippi* with either USS *Powhatan* or USS *Susquehanna* (NHHC 42760.)

COMMODORE MATTHEW PERRY, C. 1853. In the summer of 1853, Commodore Perry arrived in Japan with orders from Pres. Millard Fillmore to deliver a letter to the shogun, Tokugawa Ieyoshi. With the acquisition of Oregon (1846) and California (1848), Pacific trade was rapidly growing in importance. Like Hawaii, Japan's location made it appealing as a coaling station for steamships en route to China. (New York Public Library.)

JAPANESE PORTRAITS OF ADAMS AND PERRY, C. 1853. Merchants in Hawaii eagerly followed the negotiations in Japan, hopeful for new opportunities. From the Honolulu newspaper the *Polynesian* on May 6, 1854, comes the following account: "Dinner was served up on Lacyuer ware dishes . . . with chopsticks. [We] concluded to take a walk . . . accompanied by a couple of two-sworded silk pants Mandarins, to see that we conducted ourselves properly." (Metropolitan Museum of Art.)

"COMMODORE PERRY LANDING AT YOKU-HAMA, JAPAN," BY W. HEINE, 1853. Every earlier effort of the United States to initiate contact with Japan had failed. Perry entered Japanese waters with gifts including bourbon, a telegraph, Colt six-shooters, and a working model steam train. He also brought along an armada of 40 intimidating "black ships," making it clear that he would not take "no" for an answer. (Library of Congress.)

THE DELIVERY OF PRESIDENT FILLMORE'S LETTER BY COMMODORE PERRY, JULY 14, 1853. The Treaty of Kanagawa, negotiated literally at gunpoint, was the first trade agreement with the West that the Japanese had accepted in 300 years. It promised a supply of coal, water, and food to US warships. These same demands were made of Hawaii, coaling preceding a permanent naval station. (Library of Congress.)

THE FIRST JAPANESE EMBASSY TO THE UNITED STATES, 1860. On January 19, 1860, *Kanrin Maru* set sail for San Francisco with Manjiro "John" Nakahama aboard as translator. *Kanrin Maru*, a screw-driven steam warship, represented a Western technological advance that the Japanese were eager to show off. Pictured from left to right are Fukuzawa Yukichi, Okada Seizō, Hida Hamagorō, Konagai Gohachirō, Hamaguchi Yoemon, and Nezu Kinjirō. (National Diet Library.)

THE HAWAIIAN DELEGATION TO JAPAN, 1881. The Hawaiian monarchy was also interested in establishing a relationship with Japan. Kalākaua offered the emperor his niece as a bride for Japan's prince. The Japanese declined. How the United States would react was surely a deciding factor. Pictured from left to right are (first row, seated) Prince Yoshiaki, King David Kalākaua of Hawaii, and Tsunetani; (second row, standing) Col. Hastings Judd, chamberlain; Riyosaki; and William N. Armstrong, commissioner of Immigration, Hawaii. (HSA, PP-36-10-009.)

RICE FIELDS NEAR AIEA, C. 1890. As the Hawaiian population declined due to introduced disease, investors began purchasing taro patches to grow rice. By 1887, over 13 million pounds of rice was being produced, mostly by Chinese immigrants. However, after the 1882 Chinese Exclusion Act was passed in the United States, the Japanese began to replace them. The US government did not officially control Hawaii yet, but American business interests already did. (HHS.)

JAPANESE IMMIGRANTS ON THE CAUSEWAY TO QUARANTINE ISLAND, 1893. Japanese immigration to Hawaii began in 1885 with the arrival of 900 immigrants aboard *City of Tokio*. Chiefly, men came because jobs were available in the sugar industry. Women came as "picture brides," only seen by their husbands-to-be in photographs. (HSA, PPWD-20-4-001.)

JAPANESE "SOLDIERS" ON PARADE IN HONOLULU, 1895. The men pictured are not actual soldiers but participants in a May 11, 1895, parade in Honolulu celebrating the victory of Japan over China in the First Sino-Japanese War. Japanese merchants portrayed the army, and laborers portrayed the navy. Fireworks, wrestling, food, and other festivities began on Nuuanu Street and continued down King Street to Independence Park. A holiday was declared on the plantations, and an estimated 22,000 people participated. Non-Japanese were not permitted at the event except by invitation. The immigrants maintained strong cultural connections to their homeland, establishing their own schools and Buddhist temples. The tone of the article published in the *Hawaiian Star* shows obvious concern for the militant nature of this Japanese patriotism by reassuring newspaper readers that "the guns are all wooden." The size of the Japanese presence in Hawaii and the insular nature of the community began to raise questions about what might happen in Hawaii if the relationship between the United States and Japan deteriorated. (HSA, PP-46-6-004.)

Four

PINEAPPLE KINGS

PINEAPPLE PLANTATION LABORERS, C. 1910. Nineteenth-century Western investors noted that Hawaii's climate was ideal for growing two very profitable things: sugar and the famous, charismatic fruit that Hawaii has since been inescapably associated with–pineapple. Sanford Dole, later president of the Republic of Hawaii, was born in Hawaii. His cousin James Dole, founder of the pineapple company, arrived in 1899. (Library of Congress.)

Vast Pineapple Fields Seen from atop the Pali Looking Windward, c. 1890. The first commercially grown pineapples in Hawaii were planted by a Spanish ship pilot. Don Francisco de Paula Marín arrived in 1794 and served as an advisor to Kamehameha I, helping him to acquire weapons. For his service, he was given the land that is now Ford Island, where he also planted coffee and mangos. (HHS.)

Sugar Laborers from the Scrapbook of US Navy Submariner Joseph E. Verschelden, c. 1923. Sugar grew wild in Hawaii, but large-scale production is land- and labor-intensive. Workers were imported from China beginning in 1852 and later from Japan, Portugal, and the Philippines. Plantation work was harsh, but immigrants were fleeing political instability and extreme poverty. The foreign import tax on sugar sent to the United States was paid by the growers. This created pressure for the annexation of Hawaii by the United States. (PFSM, 1993.0025.002.)

A SUGAR MILL, EWA, C. 1900–1915. Sugar growers on the US mainland worried that the Hawaiian sugar, if not taxed as an import, would force prices down. They fiercely opposed annexation. Hawaiian foreign minister Charles Bishop proposed an alternative, avoiding the word "annexation." The US Navy could "lease" Pearl Harbor for 50 years in exchange for tax-free access to American sugar markets. (HSA, PPWD-18-14-011.)

QUEEN KALAMA HAKALELEPONI BY HENRY CHASE, 1862. While the Civil War ravaged the United States, Americans in Hawaii tried to extend their authority, mostly without permission. Following the death of Queen Hakaleleponi in 1870, all flags were supposed to go to half mast, but the US flag at the consulate did not move. The captain of USS *Jamestown* (1844) sent Marines to lower the flag—by force, if necessary. (HSA, PPWD-15-7-003.)

KING DAVID KALĀKAUA BY JAMES J. WILLIAMS, 1882. King David Kalākaua, nicknamed "the Merrie Monarch," began his reign in 1874. While acquiescing to American demands enabled him to retain his position, he was acutely aware of what Hawaii was losing and made tremendous contributions to the preservation of traditional Hawaiian culture, specifically dance and music. (HSA, PPWD-15-4.018.)

QUEEN STREET AND THE HONOLULU COURTHOUSE BY G.H. BURGESS, 1857. The election of Kalākaua was violently contested. Queen Emma, Kamehameha IV's widow, had been nearly unanimously voted in, but Kalākaua was seen as more likely to cooperate with the US Navy. When the popular vote was arbitrarily overturned, a riot broke out. American warships quickly sent 150 sailors and Marines to take control with a Gatling gun. (HSA, PP-38-1-016.)

KAIMILOA, 1887. Kalākaua's steamer *Kaimiloa* was a far cry from Kamehameha's powerful fleet, obsolete at the time of her construction. Although she was armed, she could not compete with any US or European vessel. A German gunboat actually took a shot across her bow when she arrived in Samoa, and when the Germans declared war on any Samoans who were friendly with the Hawaiians, *Kaimiloa* was called home. (HSA, PPWD-17-8-008.)

TWO KINGS ABOARD *KAIMILOA*, 1887. Kalākaua was aware that his power was being taken and sought to prove himself by making overtures to Hawaii's neighbors. Samoa's cultural similarities made it a good potential ally. Unfortunately, the Germans had interests in Samoa and opposed Kalākaua's efforts. A ceremony aboard *Kaimiloa* celebrated the short 1887 alliance between Samoa and Hawaii. Pictured are the two kings, Kalākaua and Malietoa, with their entourages and sailors. (HSA, PPWD-17-8-004.)

THE HONOLULU RIFLES, C. 1880. By the end of the 19th century, the 300,000 native Hawaiians had fallen to 30,000. American merchants owned roughly four times the land and property of Hawaiians. Despite its name, the Hawaiian League was comprised entirely of wealthy foreigners, notably Sanford Dole. When the League sent Kalākaua a list of demands, it had the Honolulu Rifles deliver it. (HSA, PP-52-1-019.)

KING KALĀKAUA AND ROBERT LOUIS STEVENSON, C. 1889. The 1887 Bayonet Constitution stripped citizenship as necessary for voting, instead requiring ownership of property and income. Hawaiians no longer controlled their kingdom. Attempts to restore Kalākaua's power met with USS *Adams* (1874) landing four boats of Marines. Having very little real authority, Kalākaua dedicated himself to the preservation of Hawaiian arts and culture. (HSA, PP-96-14-008-1889.)

KING KALĀKAUA ABOARD USS CHARLESTON, 1890. USS *Charleston* (C-2) took King Kalākaua to the mainland in 1890 for medical assistance when he suffered a stroke. Doctors were unable to help him. Pictured with Kalākaua aboard *Charleston* are the officers of the warship, Rear Adm. George Brown (fourth from right) and Capt. George C. Remey (third from right). His aides, Maj. Robert Hoapili Baker and Col. George W. Macfarlane, stand directly behind the king. (HSA, PPWD-15-4-014.)

MANNING THE YARDS IN HONOR OF QUEEN KAPIOLANI, CONSORT OF KALĀKAUA, 1887. The naval custom of "manning the rails" to render honors evolved from "manning the yards" during the age of sail. Pictured here are USS *Atlanta* (1884) sailors manning the yards in honor of Queen Kapiolani upon her arrival in New York City while on her way to England for Queen Victoria's 1887 Golden Jubilee. (HSA, PP-97-15-009.)

QUEEN LILI'UOKALANI, LAST REIGNING MONARCH OF THE HAWAIIAN KINGDOM, C. 1891. One of the first actions of Hawaii's last reigning monarch, Queen Lili'uokalani, was to draft a new constitution restoring voting rights to her people. In response, the Hawaiian League formed the "Committee of Safety" to "protect the property" of Americans. A group including Marines from USS *Boston* (1884) removed the queen from power. US president Grover Cleveland had not approved this. He called it an "act of war" and blocked requests for annexation. Lili'uokalani chose not to prevent her own overthrow, fearing resistance would cost her supporters their lives. She was put under house arrest. In 1895, she was accused of having been involved in a failed attempt to restore the monarchy, of which she said she had no knowledge. Once again, an American warship's presence, this time USS *Philadelphia* (C-4), forced the queen to formally abdicate. While imprisoned, Lili'uokalani composed many songs and translated important Hawaiian history into English. She was released from house arrest in 1896 and spent the rest of her life protesting the wrongs done to her country and herself. (HSA, PPWD-16-3-028.)

USS Boston's Overthrow of the Hawaiian Monarchy, 1893. USS *Boston* (1884) came to Hawaii as part of a prospective Pacific Squadron commanding officer's cruise in 1892. She played a key role in the January 1893 overthrow of the Hawaiian monarchy. Pictured is *Boston's* landing force occupying the Arlington Hotel grounds on January 17, 1893. Comdr. Lucien Young is in command of the troops. This site was formerly the childhood home of Lili'uokalani and Bernice Pauahi-Bishop. (HSA, PP-36-3-002.)

Petitioning for the Restoration of the Monarchy, 1893. Influential Hawaiians reached out to petition Rep. James Blount of Georgia, who had opposed annexation. Blount investigated the overthrow but could not do much. Pictured from left to right are Sam M. Kaaukai, J.W. Bipikane, H.S. Swinton, J.K. Kaulia, L.W.P. Kanealii, Joseph Nawahi, John Sam Kekukahiko, S.K. Aki, J.A. Cummins, D.W. Pua, John K. Prendergast, John E. Bush, A.K. Palekaluhi, John Mahiai Kaneakua, J.K. Kaunamano, F.S. Keiki, J. Kekipi, John L. Kaulukou, and J.K. Merseburg. (Library of Congress.)

THE COMMITTEE OF PUBLIC SAFETY, 1893. The "Committee of Public Safety" was a misleading name for a group of merchants taking over Hawaii for profit. Pictured are Henry E. Cooper, chairman (center), and, clockwise from top, Theodore F. Lansing, Henry Waterhouse, Lorrin A. Thurston, Ed Suhr, F.W. McChesney, John Emmeluth, William R. Castle, William O. Smith, J.A. McCandless, C. Bolte, W.C. Wilder, and Andrew Brown. A key figure, though not an official member, was Sanford Dole. (HSA, PP-36-3-001.)

PROVISIONAL GOVERNMENT OF THE REPUBLIC OF HAWAII, 1893. Americans numbered only 4,000 in Hawaii in 1900, in comparison to 46,500 Japanese and Chinese and 39,000 Hawaiians. However, the cabinet of the Provisional Government of the Republic of Hawaii (formerly the Committee of Public Safety) did not actually allow any sort of legitimate elections, as "Republic" might imply. The Executive Council is, from left to right, James A. King, Sanford B. Dole, W.O. Smith, and P.C. Jones. (HSA, PP-28-7-012.)

ROBERT WILLIAM KALANIHIAPO WILCOX, 1889. Robert William Kalanihiapo Wilcox, the "Iron Duke of Hawaii," led two failed rebellions in Hawaii, the first in 1889 to force Kalākaua to reject the Bayonet Constitution of 1887. Wilcox's father was an American and his mother was Hawaiian. Wilcox would also lead the 1895 revolt against the Republic of Hawaii under Dole. In this photograph, he is wearing an Italian military uniform at the Honolulu police station. (University of Hawaii at Manoa.)

REPUBLIC OF HAWAII SOLDIERS ON THE ROOF OF IOLANI PALACE, JANUARY 7, 1895. The royalists of Wilcox's 1895 rebellion were seriously outgunned by the Republic. A guerilla campaign proved impossible to sustain. Wilcox was tried for treason (the second time), found guilty, and sentenced to death. Remarkably, Wilcox was not executed. He was later elected the first delegate to the US Congress for the Territory of Hawaii. (HSA, PP-53-3-004.)

QUEEN LILI'UOKALANI
AND HER ENTOURAGE AT
WASHINGTON PLACE, 1898.
Queen Lili'uokalani traveled
to Washington, DC, in June
1897 to meet with President
McKinley. Unable to prevent
annexation, she filed a lawsuit
claiming $450,000 in damages
for the loss of her throne
and property. Pictured are
Queen Lili'uokalani, Princess
Kaiulani, Prince David
Kawananakoa, and their
supporters. Note the feather
kāhili (royal standards) around
the room. (USAMH, 7193.)

THE LOWERING OF THE HAWAIIAN FLAG, 1898. On February 15, 1898, USS *Maine* (1889) was blown up in Cuba. The Spanish-American War would give the United States control over the Philippines and Guam. Firmly entrenched in the Pacific, it was seen as necessary for the United States to finally take Hawaii. Despite tens of thousands of signatures collected in protest, President McKinley approved the annexation on July 7, 1898. (HSA, PP-35-8-017.)

Five

MOVING IN

PEARL LOCHS BY C.J. LIDGATE, 1873. Around the 12th century, chief Keaunui of Ewa cut a channel near the Pearl River. This was the beginning of Pearl Harbor. Prior to dredging, large ships could not pass over the reef to enter, though it was observed that the lochs were 36–42 feet deep. The land was owned by many powerful people, including the Bishops and the Dillinghams. (Library of Congress.)

MAJ. GEN. JOHN M. SCHOFIELD BY C.M. BELL, 1860. Major General Schofield was assigned the task of surveying Pearl Harbor in 1873, long before the US government owned it. He stated, "[One harbor] can be made to satisfy all the conditions necessary in time of war, providing water deep enough for the largest vessels . . . around Rabbit [Ford] Island." He pushed immediate action, stating, "When war has begun it will be too late." (Library of Congress.)

US ARMY SOLDIERS IN HAWAII, 1898. The Spanish-American War and its aftermath was a significant reason for the United States deciding to annex Hawaii when it did. The mess line of the 1st New York Volunteer Infantry is pictured between August and October 1898. (USAMH, 1838.)

JAPANESE CRUISER NANIWA, 1898. Fearing the United States' anti-Asian policies would be used against Japanese who had already immigrated to Hawaii, Japan sent the cruiser *Naniwa* to protest annexation. The British also got into a position to defend their citizens if violence erupted. The captain of *Naniwa*, future Fleet Admiral Togo Heihachirō, allowed an escaped Japanese prisoner convicted of murder to stay aboard his ship, nearly causing a diplomatic incident. (NHHC, 74395.)

CAMP MCKINLEY, C. 1905. Assistant Secretary of the Navy (and future president) Theodore Roosevelt observed at the time "a very real present danger of war." The United States paid Japan $75,000 to settle the issue, but it already seemed that a Pacific war might begin in Hawaii. Four days after annexation, the 1st New York Volunteer Infantry Regiment established Camp McKinley at Kapiolani Park near Diamond Head volcano. (USAMH, 54.)

THE INAUGURATION OF GOV. S.B. DOLE AT IOLANI PALACE, JUNE 15, 1900. The short-lived Republic of Hawaii lasted less than four years before Hawaii was annexed by the United States—not that this changed much. "President" Sanford Dole would also be Hawaii's first territorial governor. (HSA, PP-36-6-003.)

AIEA SUGAR MILL LOOKING TOWARD PEARL HARBOR BY TAI SING LOO, C. 1919. The Navy pursued funds to dredge Pearl Harbor, but requests were denied because it did not own the land. Owners received "reasonable" offers of $16,800 (about $600,000). However, Pearl Harbor was "worth its weight in sugar," and no one would sell. Eventually, the government condemned the land and seized it. Lawsuits continued against this seizure until 1993. (HHS.)

US Navy Coaling in Honolulu, 1905. The first regular US Navy presence in Hawaii was a coaling station established in 1860 meant to assist ships continuing on to Japan. It was forgotten almost immediately after it was built, as resources were diverted for the Civil War. Before annexation, command of the remote and ignored Honolulu Naval Station was not a desirable position. (NHHC, NH 66257.)

Tents at Camp Very (Later Fort Armstrong), c. 1909. As more US troops began arriving, the question of where they would be housed became increasingly difficult to answer. The only building the Navy had at this point was a coal shed from the 1860s, soon claimed by the Marines as their official barracks although it had been condemned 40 years earlier. (USAMH, 95.)

"EXODUS FROM CHINATOWN," JANUARY 20, 1900. The new government faced an unexpected crisis when a young Chinese man died unexpectedly from bubonic plague. The Board of Health quarantined Chinatown and planned a controlled burn for January 20, 1900. However, a shift in the wind caused a church to catch fire, and its spire fell on another building. The fire burned for 17 days, consuming 38 acres of Honolulu. (HSA, PPWD-2-12-013.)

CHINATOWN BUBONIC PLAGUE DISINFECTION STATION, 1900. At disinfection stations, residents were stripped naked and inspected for insects. This measure, draconian and humiliating, was also racist. White citizens were not stripped in public and did not have to fight for compensation for their lost property. In all, 61 people died from the plague. (HSA, PP-17-12-006.)

HONOLULU NAVAL STATION, 1904. In the early 20th century, Comdr. John Merry initially received so little support running the US naval station in Honolulu that he sent a plea to the mainland requesting "something other than a bicycle" to get around. Another problem was a shortage of water—the river was only full when it rained. Pictured is USS *Bennington* (PG-4) at left. (NHHC, NH 102745.)

USS IROQUOIS (AT-46). When the naval station tug, USS *Iroquois* (AT-46), needed repairs, the commandant sent it to Mare Island, California, despite consuming 200 tons of coal on the trip. He protested that work done by "the locals" in Hawaii was always over budget, behind schedule, and of poor quality. Locals protested that the Navy would not meet demands for reasonable wages or working hours. (NHHC, NH 70882.)

HAWAII TERRITORIAL SENATE, 1907. Careful organization and planning led to Hawaiians suddenly becoming the majority in the first territorial legislature. Unfortunately, they were met with stiff resistance from those who had previously been in control. The outcome was that the legislature had many legitimate grievances on its agenda and not enough support or resources to accomplish much. (HSA, PPWD-4-4-007.)

PRINCE KUHIO, C. 1920. Prince Jonah Kuhio sought to improve conditions for Hawaiians by making the transition from royal family member to elected representative. Japan was at war with its neighbors in the early 1900s, and it seemed possible that Hawaii would be attacked. Kuhio supported the US Navy's efforts at Pearl Harbor and helped push $2.7 million for the construction of defenses through the Territorial Congress. (HSA, PP-97-2-018.)

USS Connecticut (BB-18) Leads the Great White Fleet to Sea, December 1907. The US War Department actively planned for a war against Japan over the Pacific beginning in 1906. The Navy's Asiatic and Pacific Squadrons combined into the US Pacific Fleet on April 15, 1907. To further demonstrate the power of the US and discourage Japan, Pres. Theodore Roosevelt sent his "Great White Fleet" on a cruise around the world. (NHHC, 92067.)

Pineapples Piled on a Battleship's Deck, 1908. During the Great White Fleet's visit to Honolulu in July of 1908, fresh fruit was taken aboard. This image is from the collection of Chief Quartermaster John Harold. (NHHC 106099.)

THE GREAT WHITE FLEET DOCKED IN HONOLULU, 1908. The 16 battleships of the Great White Fleet and their escorts sailed around the globe between December 1907 and February 1909. Despite the grand spectacle they were creating, the Navy had just 90 ships at this time, over a third of them obsolete (including the fleet's ships). Still, Roosevelt's mission to display US power to the world was considered a success. (HHS.)

USS MINNESOTA (BB-22) BRINGS THE FLEET MAIL FROM HONOLULU, JULY 1908. Protesting the Navy's show of force, Queen Lili'uokalani left before the fleet arrived. On July 16, 1908, the lead ship rounded Diamond Head. Pineapple and sugar growers entertained officers. Visitors witnessing holes dug for gun emplacements at Pearl Harbor commented that it was "a shame to spoil such a lovely spot." (NHHC, NH 105997.)

US Navy Sailors on Waikiki Beach, 1908. A race boat crew from one of the fleet's battleships rests at Waikiki Beach, Oahu, Hawaii Territory, on July 19, 1908. Their ship is probably USS *Connecticut* (BB-18), as the officer in the left-center background is Midshipman Robert R.M. Emmet. The photograph states that this was the winning crew that day. (NHHC, 106181.)

Japanese Children aboard USS *Kansas* (BB-21), October 1908. At one picnic during the fleet's visit to Japan, a young Japanese sailor, the future Admiral Togo, was tossed in the air and caught in a blanket. An American ensign also present that day, future admiral William F. "Bull" Halsey, later said "if we had known what the future held, we would not have caught him." (NHHC, NH 82772.)

FLAGSHIP OF THE GREAT WHITE FLEET USS CONNECTICUT (BB-18) OFF HONOLULU, 1908. Each leg of the 14-month voyage culminated in a pageant at a new port (26 in all). At night, the battleships would be dramatically lit up, as seen in this rare photograph. When the Great White Fleet arrived in Hawaii, it was not possible for the ships to sail into Pearl Harbor, and the 16 vessels would not fit in Honolulu Harbor. The fleet dropped anchor in open water, and four ships had to travel 7-miles to Maui to refuel. Having "the Gibraltar of the Pacific" only eight miles away and yet still inaccessible helped to push forward the Navy's requests for funding to dredge and build facilities. The stark white paint that gave the fleet its name did pose an interesting problem. Though their objective was to be seen, officers recognized that in wartime, being so visible would be a problem. This began the Navy's conversion to haze gray, which has been used ever since. (HHS.)

Six

PEARL HARBOR
BETWEEN THE WARS

WALTER DILLINGHAM'S HAWAIIAN DREDGING, C. 1911. The US Navy eventually succeeded in dredging Pearl Harbor, but not with the intention of letting anyone else use it. Fishermen and commercial interests were immediately cut out. One of the first dredges to arrive on site in 1903 was cut from its moorings in a storm, and locals saw this as a portent of trouble to come. (HSA, PNL-195-06254.)

REVIEWING STAND AT THE OPENING OF PEARL HARBOR, DECEMBER 14, 1911. USS *California* (ACR-6) was the first large vessel to transit the channel entrance to Pearl Harbor, officially opening the port. On board was Sanford Dole, the first and last president of the Republic of Hawaii, and Queen Lili'uokalani, the last monarch of the Kingdom of Hawaii. The two may have had an uneasy meeting, as they were brought together by the power that had seized Hawaii from both of them, the US military. Queen Lili'uokalani was accompanied by Col. Curtis Piehu Iaukea and his wife and Mr. and Mrs. E.D. Tenney (of Matson Shipping and Castle & Cooke), both possibly seated near her (above the children, fourth from left) in this photograph. (HSA, PPWD-16-3-009.)

MAKAPUU LIGHTHOUSE INTERIOR, 1909. The Makapuu Lighthouse possesses one of the largest lenses in a lighthouse in the United States—a hyper-radiant lens. Although the tower is only 46 feet high, the light sits on a cliff 420 feet above the sea. The 115,000-candlepower light can be seen for 28 miles. The lighthouse was first lit in 1909. (US Coast Guard.)

COALING STATION AT PEARL HARBOR, C. 1919. By the outbreak of World War I, the US Navy had already begun the conversion from coal to fuel-oil-burning ships. Multiple discoveries of oil in Texas hastened the growth of the American petroleum industry in the 1920s. USS *Texas* (BB-35) was the last American battleship to be built with coal-fired boilers. It was converted to burn fuel oil in 1925. (Library of Congress.)

THE 1ST US INFANTRY ARRIVES AT SCHOFIELD BARRACKS, C. 1912. The first US Army base on Oahu, Fort Shafter, was established in 1907. An ordinance depot and a hospital (later moved to become Tripler Hospital) were constructed in 1917. Cavalry drill grounds were located at what is now Wheeler Army Airfield, which would be modified for planes in 1922. (Tropic Lightning Museum, 96.06.02-06.)

CAVALRY TAKE THEIR HORSES FOR A SWIM, C. 1920. Schofield quickly became a key training area for the US Army, which was also navigating one of the most dramatic transitions in the history of warfare—from horses to motor vehicles. (Tropic Lightning Museum, 12.03.01.072.)

MEN WITH A 12-INCH M-1890-M1 RAILWAY MORTAR, FORT KAMEHAMEHA, C. 1925. "The war to end all wars" had little effect on Hawaii. Around 1,000 men from Hawaii served in World War I. Most of those sent to Oahu were put to work on various construction projects. The large coastal batteries were never needed, though men were taught how to fire and maintain them. (USAMH, 2084.)

A 155-MM GUN IN ACTION, KOLEKOLE PASS, C. 1917. Schofield Barracks sits at the foot of the Waianae mountains and was defended on its western edge (northeast of Pu'u Kumakali'i) by Battery Kole Kole (1941-1944). This battery consisted of two 240-mm howitzers. One of the most powerful field artillery weapons of their time, these guns were able to fire 360-pound high explosive projectiles over 25,000 yards. (USAMH, 466.)

SMS *Geier* with Her Boilers on Fire, Honolulu, February 4, 1917. During World War I, the German merchant ship SMS *Geier* pulled into then-neutral Hawaii for repairs. Japanese battleships cruised back and forth waiting for her to come out. Seeing this problem, the US government issued an ultimatum demanding that the Germans either leave on a certain date or stay for the duration of the war. On the day *Geier* was supposed to depart, a large crowd of spectators, many Japanese, gathered to see what would happen. *Geier*'s captain decided to accept internment. For a time, the Germans were treated as guests in Honolulu, but when the United States entered the war, *Geier*'s crew decided to set her on fire and destroy her. Their attempt was unsuccessful, and Rear Adm. George R. Clark was given credit for taking the vessel as a war prize. The US Navy commissioned her as USS *Schurz* and put her on convoy duty. The German sailors became prisoners of the US Army at Schofield. (National Archives, 165-WW-272C-007.)

USS MARYLAND (ACR-9/CA-8), 1915. During maneuvers off Honolulu on March 25, 1915, the submarine USS F-4 (SS-23) sank at a depth of 306 feet 1.5 miles from the harbor. The response to this disaster tested the Navy's capacity to respond in a crisis. USS *Maryland* (ACR-8/CA-8), which brought the equipment used to raise *F-4*, was photographed by H.L. "Shorty" Bell, who served aboard. (PFSM, 1978.0001.002.)

DIVER JACK AGRAZ SURFACES FOLLOWING A 215-FOOT DIVE, 1915. To save the 21 men aboard *F-4*, US Navy divers shattered multiple diving records. Divers had not exceeded 200 feet in 1915. The pressure at 300 feet is over 130 pounds per square inch, and the visibility is nonexistent. The air had to be manually pumped down via a hose. (PFSM, 2020.6.8.)

CHIEF GUNNER'S MATE FRANK WILLIAM CRILLEY (1883–1947). Crilley received the Medal of Honor for rescuing another diver trapped in his own lifeline while trying to reach F-4 (SS-23). He returned to service multiple times after retiring, assisting with difficult operations, including USS S-51 (SS-162), USS S-4 (SS-109), and USS Squalus (SS-192). In the case of Squalus, 33 survivors were rescued. (PFSM, 1997.7.2.)

F-4 (SS-23) IN DRYDOCK AFTER SALVAGE, 1915. F-4 is seen here in drydock after being raised. The pontoons used in the raising are seen on either side of the vessel. The submarine is lying on her port side and is surrounded by the men who participated in the salvage operation. The investigating board concluded that seawater had seeped into the submarine's batteries, resulting in an explosion. (PFSM, 1989.3268.)

F-4 (SS-23) Crew, 1915. Crewmembers of USS *F-4* (SS-23) are marked with Xs in this photograph. All 21 men aboard lost their lives, but one man was standing watch at the time and survived. Four divers including Crilley were awarded the Medal of Honor, rarely given outside of combat. Only four of the dead could be identified; the 17 others were buried together in Arlington National Cemetery. (PFSM, 2020.6.17.)

Wreckage of Pearl Harbor's First Drydock, February 19, 1913. For Pearl Harbor's first drydock, Congress permitted only a 620-foot dock, half of what was requested, arguing that it would never be necessary to work on battleships in Hawaii. Locals warned that the site was dangerous and construction would anger the gods. Workers observed phenomena they thought were sabotage, but the actual danger was far worse. (HSA, PNL-197-06322.)

DRYDOCK NO. 1 AT PEARL HARBOR, C. 1918–1919. While still under construction, the drydock exploded due to the underground hydrostatic pressure. Walter Dillingham described the sight: "In five minutes, several million feet of timber were broken into kindling wood, pumps, hoisting engines, concrete mixers, derricks, locomotives—tangled mass of ruins and two years'

ANOTHER VIEW OF DRYDOCK NO. 1 AT PEARL HARBOR, C. 1918–1919. Arguments over whose fault it was continued for two years. An entirely different design was necessary. Concrete was first laid in slabs and then carefully positioned and bound together. Costs totaled more than $20 million

work destroyed in less time than it takes to relate the catastrophe." One thousand workers were immediately laid off, and what remained of the project was a $4-million pile of garbage. (PFSM, 2019.197-198.)

by August 21, 1919, when Drydock No. 1 was finally complete. Better engineering and a kahuna's blessing allowed the new drydock to operate just fine. (PFSM, 2019.197-198.)

BUFFALO SOLDIERS, 1918. The 25th Infantry Regiment, an all-Black unit of "Buffalo Soldiers," was stationed in Hawaii between 1913 and 1918. They participated in the development of Hawaii Volcanoes National Park, measuring lava within the summit of Kīlauea volcano. They were also among the first to stay at Kilauea Military Camp. One group volunteered its time to build a high-elevation, 30-mile trail connecting the summits of Kīlauea and Mauna Loa volcanoes. (USAMH, 3537.)

THE WAR MEMORIAL NATATORIUM, C. 1927. Constructed during a 1920s building boom partially funded by sugar companies, the natatorium, which sits in ruin today, was once an important public site. When it opened on August 24, 1927, Olympic Gold medalist and "father of surfing" Duke Kahanamoku dove into the pool for the first ceremonial swim. The natatorium, part memorial and part community hub, cleverly tied American patriotism to centuries of Hawaiian swimming tradition. (HSA, PNM-289-19937.)

USS Alton (Former Chicago) as a Receiving Ship, c. 1930. One solution to housing problems was utilizing obsolete ships. One of the Navy's first steel ships, USS *Chicago* (1885), was decommissioned at Pearl Harbor in 1923. Chicago was renamed *Alton* (IX-5), freeing the name for USS *Chicago* (CA-29), and was used as barracks until 1935. (PFSM, 2020.27.3.)

Chester Nimitz on USS *Chicago* (1885), Flagship of the Submarine Force, c. 1921. In 1921, Capt. Thomas Hart led 10 subs from the East Coast to the Philippines. Every submarine broke down at some point during his cruise, emphasizing the need for repair facilities in the Pacific. A promising young lieutenant commander, Chester Nimitz, the future fleet admiral, was already in Hawaii constructing a submarine base. (NHHC, NHF-112-B.01.)

HARRY BARLOW ABOARD USS *R-5* (SS-82), C. 1924. Early submarines were derisively referred to as "pigboats" in reference to their unsanitary condition. The *Honolulu Advertiser* wrote of the arrival of the first R-class submarines to Pearl Harbor, referring to them as "sewer pipes discharging men." (PFSM, 1993.25.)

LOADING FISH, C. 1924. Hawaii quickly became an important proving ground for advancing submarine technology. Here, sailors aboard USS *R-5* (SS-82) are pictured loading "fish" (torpedoes) at Lahaina Roads, Maui. The area was commonly used by the Navy for gun and torpedo practice. (PFSM, 1993.25.)

STUCK ON A REEF, C. 1924. Here, USS *R-11* (SS-88) receives assistance from *R-5* (SS-82) after becoming stuck on a reef. Extensive dredging had made the entrance to Pearl Harbor easily accessible, but vessels that ventured around the neighboring islands still got themselves into trouble. (PFSM, 1993.25.)

DESTROYERS, C. 1925. The year 1925 brought 137 US Navy ships to Hawaii. Pictured are destroyers moored together at Pearl Harbor in about 1925. From left to right are USS *Stoddert* (DD-302), USS *Percival* (DD-298), USS *John Francis Burnes* (DD-299), USS *Farragut* (DD-300) and USS *Somers* (DD-301). *Percival* was named for "Mad Jack" Percival of the infamous 1826 "Battle of Honolulu." (NHHC, NH 82564.)

ESCAPE TANK - SUB-BASE

DIVE TRAINING TOWER BY TAI SING LOO, C. 1934. Built in 1932, the 30-meter-tall submarine diver training tower is 100 feet deep and 18 feet in diameter. It holds 209,331 gallons of water. There are locks at various depths from which escape can be attempted. At the time the tower was constructed, nothing resembling modern diving equipment existed. The training was conducted using a primitive rebreather called the Momsen lung. The original photograph is colorized with bright blue and green watercolor. (PFSM, 2019.251.)

WIRELESS TOWERS, C. 1931. Communication between Hawaii and the US mainland presented many challenges. In the foreground of this 1931 photograph are minesweepers USS *Seagull* (AM-30), USS *Ortolan* (AM-45), and USS *Widgeon* (AM-22), which were later converted to submarine rescue vessels. Behind them is the submarine USS *S-25* (SS-130). In the far background, it is possible to see water towers and wireless towers, the first constructed on Oahu. (PFSM, 1990.32.11.)

QUARRY POINT, 1920. Quarry Point in 1920 shows a small number of tents and buildings. Construction began on the piers in 1918. Under the war program, existing facilities were expanded to the limits of the land available. Note the Oahu Rail & Land Company rail. In the upper left is Salt Lake. A considerable landfill was required to make the cactus-filled swamp useable. (PFSM, 2019.200.3.)

May, 1935

SUBMARINE BASE PEARL HARBOR (QUARRY POINT), 1935. A tremendous increase in incoming vessels necessitated the rapid expansion of housing and fuel storage. Much of this construction took place between 1920 and 1935. This photograph shows Kuahua Island's (Quarry Point) evolution into the submarine base at Pearl Harbor's Southeast Loch. The receiving ship, USS *Alton* (ex-*Chicago*), which served as temporary housing, is the vessel with two ramps leading up to it. Fuel storage tanks are visible in the background. Note that the diver training tower has been constructed along with barracks and a swimming pool. Roads, piers, and parking have also been improved. *Alton* was sold for scrap soon after this photograph was taken. The old ship was in such poor condition that she never completed her final voyage from Honolulu to San Francisco. She instead foundered and sank in the middle of the Pacific. (PFSM, 2022.48.15.)

Seven

THE HONOLULU HOP

SKYLARK SOARS OVER OAHU, 1910. Only a few years after the Wright brothers' first successful flight, a Curtiss P-18 biplane arrived in Hawaii by steamer. Spectators watched in awe as the plane, piloted by Bud Masters, took to the air. The event drew a crowd of over 3,000 to witness the "bird man" in action. A feat for the era, he flew 500 feet over Moanalua Polo Field, Oahu, in his plane, christened *Skylark*. (HSA, PP-3-11-009.)

BELLOWS FIELD, 1917. Bellows Field was created in 1917 as the Waimanalo Military Reservation on a leased former sugar plantation. It was renamed in 1933 for World War I hero Lt. Franklin Barney Bellows. The first runway was constructed of 10-foot-deep crushed coral and measured 75 feet by 983 feet. (USAMH, 2625.)

SEAPLANE RAMPS, 1921. The seaplane station at Pearl Harbor, pictured on November 16, 1921, moved to Ford Island in 1923. Canvas hangars protected two HS-2L flying boats and two N-9 float planes salvaged from World War I. Seaplanes had trouble landing around Ford Island, but dealing with coral was preferable to trying to land anywhere else. Badly behaved servicemen were assigned to clear plants from future runways as punishment. (Courtesy of the Pearl Harbor Aviation Museum.)

COMDR. JOHN RODGERS'S PN-9, 1925. Prior to 1925, no aircraft had flown from California to Honolulu. Comdr. John Rodgers was the second naval officer to qualify as an aviator, graduating from the Wright Flying School in 1911. He gathered a crew to undertake this challenge on August 31, 1925. Overly confident, Rodgers radioed Hawaii's governor and said they would arrive the next day. Crowds had already formed when an ominous message was received from the aviators: "plane low on gasoline." "The Flight Is Doomed!" the *Honolulu Advertiser* declared. A massive search was launched. Unbeknownst to everyone, the plane had landed safely on the ocean. The crew was able to listen to their radio but could not transmit. When they realized they would not be found, they stripped fabric from the bottom wing of their PN-9 to fashion a sail. (Courtesy of the Pearl Harbor Aviation Museum.)

THE LUCKY CREW OF RODGERS'S PN-9, 1925. Kauai represented their final chance, so Rodgers set course for the island. Ten days after they should have arrived in Hawaii, the crew of the PN-9 was out of food and water and trailed by sharks. Fatefully, the submarine *R-4* spotted them. Rodgers asked the submarine for food, water, and cigarettes, intending to sail the rest of the way into port. Thinking the aviators were delirious and insane, the sub's commanding officer almost had them physically removed, but Rodgers acquiesced and allowed the submarine to be their "pilot." Rodgers insisted on a picture with his crew before they cleaned up. Pictured are Lt. B.J. Connell, pilot; W.H. Bowlin, aviation mechanic's mate first class; S.R. Pope, second pilot; and O.G. Stantz, radio operator. (NHHC, NH 65744.)

USS *R-14* (SS-91) under Sail by Albion Ross, 1921. The PN-9 was not the only strange vessel sailing to Hawaii in the 1920s. Submarine *R-14* was looking for a missing tugboat when she ran out of fuel 100 miles from Hilo. The crew discovered her reserve tanks were empty and then encountered issues with their radio. Rescue seemed unlikely, so the crew began making a sail from hammocks. Pipe bunk frames lashed together made the foreyard. The watch's log recorded, "Underway on starboard tack steering 320 degrees true making for Hilo Bay, speed estimated one knot." Not satisfied, the crew made a mainsail and a mizzen sail using officers' blankets and curtain rods. The improvised square-rigger limped into Hilo on May 17, 1921, at approximately two knots. Pictured are H.D. Wilkinson; Lieutenant Douglas (hatless), acting commanding officer, and Quartermaster's Mate 2nd Class Frank Joseph Unger (uppermost). (PFSM, 2021.66.55.)

BIRD OF PARADISE LANDS AT WHEELER FIELD, 1927. The Army had also been preparing for a transpacific flight, hoping to succeed before the Navy did. Two planes were chosen. The first, a trimotor Fokker C-2 name *Bird of Paradise*, successfully completed its flight and landed at Wheeler, where it was greeted by cavalry and crowds, as seen in the cover image of this book. (HSA, PP-3-10-004.)

THE WRECK OF *CITY OF OAKLAND* ON MOLOKAI, 1927. The Army's second pioneering airplane, the single-engine Travel Air 5000 *City of Oakland*, was forced to make an emergency landing on Molokai. Flown by Ernie Smith and Emory Bronte, it crashed near Norman Maguire's Kamalo Ranch on July 15, 1927. (HSA, PP-3-1405.)

THE "DISASTER DERBY," 1927.
Although military fliers had already successfully flown to Hawaii, James Dole proposed a transoceanic race for this historical "first" advertised as the "Dole Derby" with a prize of $25,000. On August 16, 1927, eight planes departed Oakland. Three would-be entrants had already died in crashes en route to the starting line. Only two reached Hawaii: *Woolaroc* and *Aloha*. (Courtesy of the Pearl Harbor Aviation Museum.)

MRS. JENSEN AND JAMES D. DOLE AWAIT THE ARRIVAL OF SURVIVING DOLE DERBY AVIATORS, 1927. Pictured here is James D. Dole with Mrs. Jensen, the wife of pilot Martin Jensen of *Aloha*, second-place finisher in the Dole Derby. None of the lost fliers were ever found, and one search plane was lost, too. In total, 10 people died trying to complete the race. The race was reported in newspapers as the "Disaster Derby" due to the fate of most of its participants. (HSA, PP-3-8-015.)

EARHART'S LOCKHEED VEGA ARRIVES IN HONOLULU ABOARD SS *LURLINE*, DECEMBER 27, 1934. Amelia Earhart crashed at Ford Island on her initial "around the world" attempt. After undergoing repairs, Earhart would embark on her final flight. Her last message to Pearl Harbor was received on July 2, 1937. A massive search followed, but she was never found. A possible wreck site, still unconfirmed, was located in February 2024. (Matson Archives.)

DUKE KAHANAMOKU AND AMELIA EARHART, 1935. Duke Kahanamoku (at this time sheriff of Honolulu) shows pioneer aviatrix Amelia Earhart how to cut up a pineapple at the Royal Hawaiian Hotel on January 2, 1935. Kahanamoku, best known for introducing surfing to the world, was also an early supporter of aviation and bestowed a lei upon the first successful commercial flight to Hawaii. (Matson Archives.)

AMERICAN CLIPPER OFF
FORD ISLAND BY PAN
PACIFIC PRESS BUREAU,
1935. On January 10,
1934, six airplanes
departed San Francisco
and successfully arrived
at Pearl Harbor just
24 hours later. Their
objective was to pioneer
air travel for tourism
purposes. Because there
was nowhere else for
them to land, most
early aircraft landed
on the water near Ford
Island, where they were
assisted by the US Navy.
(HSA, PP-1-7-008.)

HAWAII'S FIRST TOURISTS ARRIVE BY AIR, OCTOBER 1936. Pictured are the first tourists to fly to
Hawaii aboard the Pan-American Clipper with welcoming musicians and dancers. From left to
right are Richard F. Bradley, San Francisco; Zetta Averill, Aberdeen, Washington; Thomas F.
Ryan III, San Francisco; Alfred Bennet, Highstown, New Jersey; Col. Charles Bartley, Chicago;
Clara Adams, Philadelphia; and Wilbur May, Los Angeles. (HSA, PP-1-9-002.)

USS RANGER (CV-4) OFF THE COAST OF HONOLULU, MAY 29, 1935. Since aircraft of the 1930s struggled to cover distances exceeding a few hundred miles, the US military initially believed that Japan could not attack Oahu. However, the Japanese had six carriers in operation by 1939. Army officers in Hawaii pleaded for more planes, but "the defense of ocean was the Navy's business" and their requests were ignored. By the late 1930s, men who had earned their wings were rising into senior positions. They pointed out how easy it would be for carrier-based planes to approach from the northeast. Using the clouds atop the Koolau Range to conceal their presence, they could deliver a surprise attack on Pearl Harbor and neighboring airfields. These warnings were ignored by the previous generation of battleship admirals, who were unable to envision a future in which aviation would exceed the importance of ships. (Courtesy of Battleship *Missouri*.)

Eight

STEWED, SCREWED, AND TATTOOED

DRUNK SAILORS IN THE SHORE PATROL BRIG BY WAYNE MILLER, 1945.
Lt. Wayne Miller traveled to Hawaii disguised as an enlisted man to photograph sailors for a project titled "Shore Leave." Miller's caption reads, "This island whiskey is no good. . . . You should have seen the mess I saw at the Shore Patrol Brig. I got picked up for fightin'. The Shore Patrol calls them 'Pass outs.' They was lying all over the place. Out colder than a rock." (Magnum Photos.)

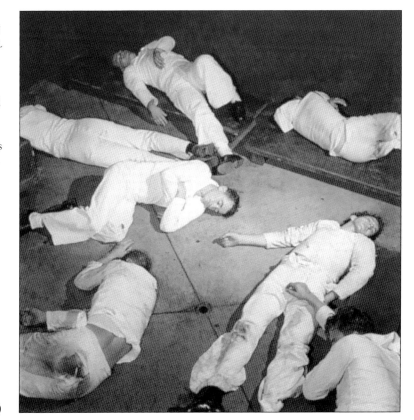

MADAM JEAN O'HARA, 1944. For reasons of "morale," military officials advocated for regulated, legal prostitution in Hawaii. Prostitutes, mostly from the mainland, were fingerprinted and issued licenses. Honolulu's most famous madam, Jean O'Hara, famously instigated a three-week strike in 1942, demanding the basic rights of American citizens for prostitutes. Prostitutes had collectively purchased $132,000 in war bonds and argued that their work was vital to the war effort. Newspapers were ordered not to print a word about the strike, but the military governor told local police that the prostitutes could "do what they liked." Some estimates suggest that during World War II, there were as many as 300 men to one woman in Honolulu. At a time when the average income was around $2,500, prostitutes were earning $25,000–40,000. When the war ended, most brothels shut down. O'Hara attempted to live a more respectable life but was later arrested for trying to murder her husband. Seen here is the cover of *Honolulu Harlot*, Jean O'Hara's tell-all book, published in 1944.

Charlie Brown, 1943. Pictured is Charlie Brown, cook aboard the submarine USS *Bowfin* (SS-287). Arcades offered sailors the opportunity to take photographs with hula girls or tropical backgrounds. These were popular souvenirs. (PFSM, 2021.31.68.)

Smith's Union Bar, 2024. Most US Navy ships during World War II had their own unofficial bars in Honolulu where the crews would go while on leave. The last of these "battleship bars" is the Smith's Union Bar, located at 19 North Hotel Street in Chinatown, formerly the official watering hole of USS *Arizona* (BB-39). The neighborhood today remains much as it ever was, although the bars now serve craft beers and fancy cocktails. (Author's photograph.)

THE GALLOPING GOOSE, C. 1920. Transportation from Pearl Harbor to Honolulu was a train called the Pineapple Express or "Galloping Goose." The train delivered sailors to a station across from Akala Park. During World War II, the point of pickup was changed to Nimitz Gate from where the submarine memorial stands today. Sailors were on "Cinderella leave," meaning they had to return to their ships by midnight. (PFSM, 2019.342.)

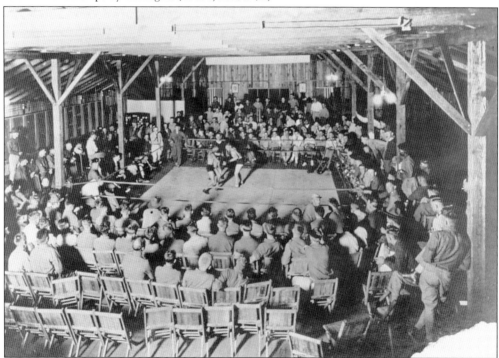

LUKE FIELD FIGHT NIGHT, 1936. Athletic contests were one popular way of keeping men entertained. Giving soldiers and sailors reasons to stay on base was the military's preferred method of preventing problems with locals. Pictured is Fight Night at Luke Field featuring Kid Parenti versus Shorty Harrison in about 1936. (USAMH, 834.)

"Crossing the Line" Aboard USS S-10 (SS-115), c. 1930. The US Navy in the 19th century underwent tremendous changes. Discipline was no longer enforced by flogging, and alcohol was no longer part of a daily ration. However, some traditions from the age of sail persisted. A line-crossing ceremony is a temporary upheaval of order and hierarchy aboard a ship, typically to boost morale. This tradition is very old—in fact, there is a record of a line-crossing ceremony conducted aboard Cook's ship HMS *Endeavor* on his 1768 voyage to the Pacific. Sailors who have never crossed the equator (pollywogs) are called before King Neptune and punished for various transgressions. The hazing, often severe, is conducted by enlisted men (shellbacks) dressed as pirates. When the ceremony ends, the pollywogs are declared shellbacks themselves. (Both, PFSM, 2004.0001.023-28.)

SAILORS ON WAIKIKI BEACH, C. 1942. Prior to widespread air travel, a visit to Hawaii simply was not possible for most people from the US mainland. However, before and during World War II, thousands of servicemen had the opportunity to enjoy everything the islands had to offer, taking up surfing, enjoying drinks on the beach, attending luaus, sightseeing waterfalls and volcanos, and trying new foods. (PFSM, 1989.3241.)

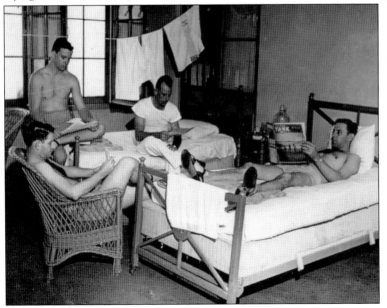

SAILORS AT THE ROYAL HAWAIIAN, C. 1942. Known as "the Pink Palace," the Royal Hawaiian was the first resort in Honolulu. It opened its doors on February 1, 1927, and by 1928, it counted over 20,000 visitors. During World War II, the Royal Hawaiian was closed to tourists and instead served as a place of rest for the military. (PFSM, 1989.3241.)

ENLISTED MEN'S BEER GARDEN, c. 1942. Pictured is the enlisted men's beer garden at the Royal Hawaiian Hotel. Officers were generally viewed as men of a higher social class and were not supposed to socialize with enlisted sailors. (PFSM, 1989.3241.18.)

BLACK SAILORS CELEBRATE V-J DAY AT CAMP CATLIN FLEET TRAINING CENTER, 1945. Black sailors and soldiers experienced segregation at home and in the military. In Hawaii, however, locals would not turn away business. The Harlem Hellfighters, renowned for their courage in World War I, became the 369th Coast Artillery in 1940. They served at Air Station Ewa and other airfields. Pictured are Steward's Mates James E. Jones and Eddie Robinson. Steward's mate was one of the only rates available to Black sailors during World War II. (NHHC, 80-G-343663.)

KAU KAU KORNER, AT THE INTERSECTION OF KAPIOLANI BOULEVARD AND KALĀKAUA AVENUE, **1945.** This famous drive-in sign showing the distance from Hawaii to home was replicated all over the Pacific by servicemembers during World War II and also during the Korean and Vietnam Wars. A personal caption on the photograph reads, "Hawaii is the crossroads of the Pacific. There is a marker that is out here on the rock." (HSA, PP-4-6-001.)

THE COOKE RANCH, C. 1940S. Over 200 private ranches and plantations volunteered to welcome servicemen for rest and relaxation, but the cattle and pineapple ranch run by George and Sophie Cooke on Molokai was something special. In the words of one sailor, "You probably cannot realize what it means to come from the type of live we lead to the cleanness, fresh air, sunlight, good food and sleep that we found as your guests. It was like an oasis . . . and to me it reawakened thoughts of what life can hold after this war is over." During World War II, 265 combat airmen and submariners were hosted by the Cookes. More than half never made it home. Sophie Cooke sent condolences to their families. Pictured below are ? Hinchey, Phoebe Cooke, C.F. Davenport, Ignatius Galantin (future admiral), ? Butler, Sophie Cooke, and ? Bunting. (Above, PFSM, 2007.0003; below, PFSM, 2019.0294.)

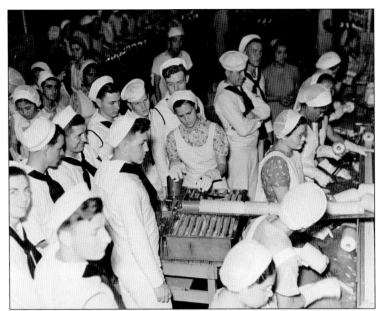

DOLE CANNERY, c. 1940s. Here, sailors watch women canning pineapple on a visit to the Dole cannery. This experience was a common "good, clean fun" excursion in the 1940s and remains popular with tourists today. (NHHC, 122502.)

PUALANI MOSSMAN, c. 1935. Pualani Mossman was considered "the most photographed girl in the Islands." She was a famous hula performer whom Matson sent to New York City in 1937 to become the face of its tourism promotion campaign. Pictured is Pualani Mossman dancing for sailors at Leilani Village, Honolulu, likely in May 1935. (HSA, PP-33-1-017.)

USS BOWFIN (SS-287) SAILORS WITH "HULA GIRL," c. 1945. Lt. Peter Van Kuran of the submarine USS *Bowfin* told his wife in a letter that Hawaii was "a paradise for plain girls." To servicemen, the presence of any women was exciting. The idea of hula girls, however, was so popular that many women who were not Hawaiian at all but from the Philippines, China, or even the mainland donned grass skirts and leis and posed for pictures. Pictured is a "hula girl" at the Royal Hawaiian in about 1945 with, from left to right, *Bowfin* crew members Joseph Knox, Bud Knoche, and E.T. Fletcher. Photographs like these could cost as much as $1 each, which made them a lucrative business during the war years. Girls would sometimes paint on their bodies where they could be touched. These girls were not Honolulu's prostitutes, and they did not want servicemen making that mistake. (PFSM, 2015.1.12.)

THE BLACK CAT CAFÉ ON HOTEL STREET BETWEEN ALAKEA AND RICHARDS STREETS, c. 1941. This photograph shows the Black Cat Café across from the Navy YMCA, a sailor leave drop-off point. Photographs of the Black Cat are often incorrectly identified as brothel lines. The restaurant boasted an arcade where men could eat, take pictures with hula girls, play slot machines, and find other opportunities to spend their money in a Coney Island atmosphere. (HSA, PP-39-6-001.)

CHIEF OF POLICE W.A. GABRIELSON, c. 1940s. According to Jean O'Hara, Honolulu police chief William Gabrielson enforced a strict set of regulations in Chinatown known as "the Ten Commandments." Prostitutes could not own cars or real estate (all of the madams did) and were not supposed to be in bars, nicer cafés, or at the beach. Here, Mayor G. Fred Wright greets Mrs. Kapolei Kila selling leis while Chief of Police W.A. Gabrielson looks on. (HSA, PP-33-10-006.)

TOKEN FROM THE NEW SENATOR HOTEL. On Hotel Street, a "hotel" was rarely a place to sleep. Under the "bullpen" system, a man paid $3 for a poker chip. A prostitute would come in and inspect him for venereal disease. If he passed, he was given three minutes. In the 1940s, just as today, "massage parlors" were a common front for prostitution. (Roger Merritt Token Collection.)

USO CLUB, C. 1940s. Ted Waggener, aviation machinist's mate third class, is photographed here with pinup girl Alyce Louis after winning a kiss at the USO Victory Club on Beretania Street. The USO club occupied a building that was formerly a Japanese department store. In 1945, eight USO locations in Honolulu served more than six million servicemembers. (HWRD, 705.)

97

EUGENE BROWNLOW, C. 1943. The word "tattoo" is of Polynesian origin, and although practiced by many societies throughout history, Europeans and Americans first saw it in the Pacific. The first Americans with tattoos were sailors. Pictured showing off his many tattoos is Eugene Brownlow, cook aboard the submarine USS *Trout* (SS-202) when she was lost on April 17, 1944. (PFSM, 1989.3333.)

OLD IRONSIDES TATTOO SHOP, 2024. Norman Keith Collins, or "Sailor Jerry," arrived in Hawaii with the Navy. In the 1930s, he opened a tattoo shop. Sailor Jerry made significant contributions to tattooing, popularized the style known as American Traditional, and mentored artists including Ed Hardy and Mike Malone. He reportedly told them to "take over his shop or burn it down" when he died. The shop still stands today. (Author's photograph.)

Nine

MANEUVERS

REAR ADM. HARRY YARNELL AND VICE ADM. KIYOSHI HASEGAWA, IMPERIAL JAPANESE NAVY, 1937. Beginning in 1923, the Navy regularly conducted large-scale exercises, termed "Fleet Problems," with an audience of foreign military leaders, including the Japanese. Fleet Problem No. 13 (1932) presented "a militaristic, Asian, island nation" (Japan) attacking Pearl Harbor. The attacking force was under the command of Rear Adm. Harry Yarnell. (NHHC, 81617.)

SUBMARINES BY TAI SING LOO, 1932. Yarnell had earned his wings as an aviator and wanted to prove the importance of air power. At dawn on a Sunday, he launched 152 planes, striking the airfields and Battleship Row with "bombs" (flour). The base was decimated. Navy brass protested that Yarnell "cheated" because his planes appeared to come from the mainland. In 1941, Japan would virtually duplicate this attack. (PFSM, 2021.70.)

SHIPS AT LAHAINA, MAUI, BY TAI SING LOO, 1932. When the fleet visited Hawaii for maneuvers, all units, except the carriers *Ranger* (CV-4), *Lexington* (CV-2), and *Saratoga* (CV-3), were berthed in Pearl Harbor without difficulty. These three vessels were forced to anchor off the shores of southern Oahu. (PFSM, 1998.2.10.)

USS New York (BB-34) by Tai Sing Loo, Pre-1926 Refit. Battleship USS *New York* (BB-34) was the lead ship of her class and the first ship to carry the 14-inch/45-caliber gun. In World War I, she was the only US ship to sink a German U-boat. Beginning in 1919, *New York* frequently hosted foreign dignitaries in the Pacific, including then-prince Hirohito of Japan. New York participated in Fleet Problems until 1937. (PFSM, 2004.1.131-134.)

Fort DeRussy's "Big Gun" Battery A, 1931. Fort DeRussy was a 19th-century Army coastal defense gun battery designed to defend Pearl Harbor and Honolulu from battleship attacks. It was built in 1909, when multiple nations including Germany and Japan were still looking to Hawaii as a port of call. The tactical shift toward air power in the years leading up to World War II meant that no battleships ever ventured close enough to test DeRussy's guns. (USAMH, 2283.)

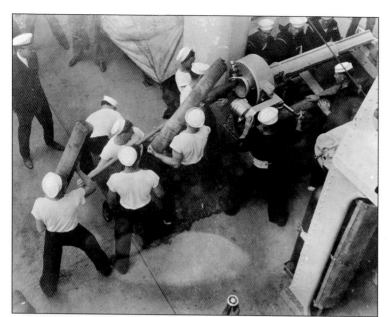

USS CINCINNATI
(CL-6), 1932.
Pictured is a gun crew
in action on a loading
machine aboard
USS *Cincinnati*
(CL-6) during
fleet maneuvers in
Hawaii in 1932.
(NHHC, 124138.)

DIAMOND HEAD, 1938. A network of tunnels was carved into the extinct Diamond Head volcano in the early 20th century. Cannon emplacements were placed atop the crater with observation posts, bunkers, and eight batteries with 12-inch M-1890-M1 coast defense mortars, anti-aircraft guns, and 8-inch guns on railway barbette carriages. Fort Ruger (renamed in 1909) was reinforced during World War II, though the guns were never fired. (USAMH, 2796.)

CONSTRUCTION OF RED HILL, 1940. One of the most controversial military sites in Hawaii began with a bribe. President Harding's secretary of interior, Albert Fall, used Pearl Harbor's need for fuel storage to mask that he had taken money. In May 1940, the Navy discovered a plot to blow oil tanks at Pearl Harbor. No damage was done, but tunneling experts from all over the country were called together. Prior to this, underground tanks had always been laid horizontally, but the engineers designed them vertically, 20 tanks each 250 feet tall and 100 feet in diameter, sunk 2,000 feet into the hill. Crewmen on outrigger canoes watched the tanks filling with water looking for bubbles with searchlights. If air could not get in, oil could not get out—or so everyone thought. Red Hill's costs totaled $43 million. About 3,900 men worked on the project, over the course of which there were 17 fatalities. The tanks, each of which holds about 12 million gallons, were discovered in 2021 to have contaminated the local water supply. (US Army Corps of Engineers.)

PRESIDENT ROOSEVELT IN HAWAII BY TAI SING LOO, 1934. President Roosevelt's official Hawaii visit in 1934 included a trip to Iolani Palace, where he urged from the balcony that the palace should be restored and open to the public. This was the first time a US president had encouraged the preservation of Hawaii's history. The caption reads, "Mr. President, this is a squid. Would you like to touch it?" (Franklin Delano Roosevelt Presidential Library and Museum.)

USS HOUSTON (CA-30) BY TAI SING LOO, 1934. USS *Houston* (CA-30) arrived in Honolulu carrying President Roosevelt in July 1934. Outrigger canoes came to meet the ship, creating an image reminiscent of the first Western arrival to the Hawaiian Islands over 150 years earlier. Roosevelt was the first sitting US president to visit Hawaii. (Franklin Delano Roosevelt Presidential Library and Museum, 48-22:3706[204].)

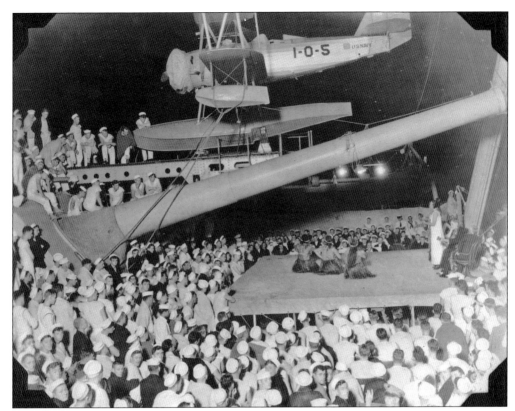

DANCERS PERFORMING ON USS NEW YORK (BB-34) ANCHORED IN HILO, MARCH 1932. A widely publicized 1931 Ala Moana assault case, the Massie Trial, resulted in the murder of an innocent local man by US Navy sailors who thought he had raped a white woman. As a result, sailors were kept aboard their ships during the 1932 fleet exercises in Hawaii. (NHHC, NHF-144.)

PEARL HARBOR FROM 2,500 FEET, MAY 26, 1944. The years 1940 and 1941 have been called "one continuous battle drill." Though the United States had repeatedly demonstrated how vulnerable its fleet could be to an air attack if the ships remained moored in one place, most who voiced this concern were dismissed. (HSA, PPFUR-2-4-036.)

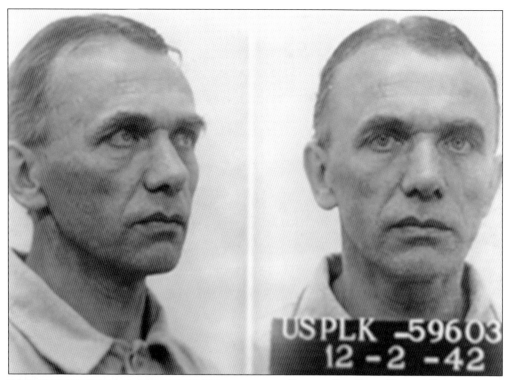

US PLK -59603
12 -2 -42

GERMAN SPY OTTO KUEHN. Spying was a family affair for the German Kuehn family. Otto Kuehn lavishly entertained military officials. His wife and daughter opened a beauty parlor where wives would come to gossip. Even his 11-year-old son collected information, dressed in a sailor suit. After the attack on Pearl Harbor, Kuehn was arrested and confessed. He avoided death when he volunteered information. The Kuehns were later deported to Germany. (National Archives.)

JAPANESE SPY TAKEO YOSHIKAWA. Japanese spy Takeo Yoshikawa was sent to Hawaii posing as a vice-consul. He rented an apartment overlooking Pearl Harbor to "enjoy the view," and flew small planes from John Rodgers Airport, taking note of fleet movements. Despite the fact that over 160,000 persons of Japanese ancestry lived in Hawaii, Yoshikawa "did not trust Japanese-Americans," believing they were more loyal to the United States than Japan. (US Naval Institute.)

MARKER FOR OPANA STATION, 2024. On December 7, 1941, Army privates George Elliott and Joseph Lockard at the SCR-270 Opana Radar Station (Kahuku Point) noticed a signal 137 miles away. Their superiors told them to ignore it, thinking it was B-17s from San Francisco. In reality, it was the Japanese. When the attack began, no one thought it was real. As Kaneohe was strafed, a sailor joked, "Here comes Tojo." (Photograph by Sarah Hausman.)

POLITICAL CARTOON BY MORAN, THE *HONOLULU ADVERTISER*, C. 1940S. Politicians on the mainland did not generally view Hawaii as part of the United States. However, propaganda needed to tie patriotic sentiment to actions that would help America win the war. Martial law would be declared in Hawaii immediately after the Japanese attack. This image of Uncle Sam, while patronizing and patriarchal, represents a shift in how Hawaii was expected to view itself. (PFSM, 1989.3308.)

TAI SING LOO, C. 1941. Official US Navy photographer Tai Sing Loo was a recognizable figure at Pearl Harbor, wearing a pith helmet and riding his three-wheeled "putt-putt." The son of immigrants, he grew up near what is now the Foster Botanical Garden and began working for the Navy in 1919. On the morning of December 7, he realized very early that something was wrong. His first instinct was to get his camera, but he also feared being mistaken for a Japanese attacker. Nevertheless, he ran toward danger, joining firefighting efforts and taking photographs as he could. During the war, Tai Sing Loo also helped break Japanese codes placed into false newspaper advertisements. After World War II, he traveled extensively, visiting friends who ranged from enlisted men to admirals. In addition to his work for the military, he photographed sports, celebrities, landscapes, and Hawaiian culture. (HSA, PP-75-5-019.)

Ten

INFAMY

JAPANESE PILOT'S VIEW OF PEARL HARBOR, DECEMBER 7, 1941. This photograph was taken from a Japanese plane during the torpedo attack on ships moored on both sides of Ford Island. The caption reads, "The enemy ships around the island have all become tempting targets for our Sea Eagles. In the upper right, clearly appear the outlines of two of our Sea Eagles who are carrying out a daring low-level attack, reminiscent of the performance of the gods." (NHHC, 80-G-30554.)

USS DOLPHIN (SS-169), DECEMBER 7, 1941. Sailors near USS *Dolphin* (SS-169) on Pier No. 4 watched Battleship Row burning. There was little else they could do. The report of the attack stated, "Fired continuously on enemy plane . . . the Duty Officer saw smoke start to come from the tail of the plane and it appeared to have crashed in the Navy Yard." Most of the Japanese planes were beyond the range of *Dolphin*'s guns. (PFSM, 1991.17.1.)

VIEW OF BATTLESHIP ROW FROM 3,000 FEET, DECEMBER 10, 1941. From left center to lower right are USS *Maryland* (BB-46), damaged, with the capsized USS *Oklahoma* (BB-37) outboard; a barge alongside *Oklahoma* supporting rescue efforts; and USS *Tennessee* (BB-43), damaged, with the sunken USS *West Virginia* (BB-48) outboard. Note dark oil streaks on the harbor surface originating from the damaged battleships. (NHHC, 80-G-387574.)

FIREFIGHTING EFFORTS, DECEMBER 7, 1941. Fires are being fought on the sunken battleship USS West Virginia (BB-48). YG-17 is at right, with her crewmen aiming two fire hoses at the flames. Assisting or standing by are a motor launch and an officer's motorboat. USS Tennessee (BB-48) is inboard of West Virginia. (NHHC, 80-G-19947.)

USS CASSIN (DD-372) AND DOWNES (DD-375), DECEMBER 7, 1941. Mahan-class destroyers USS Cassin (DD-372) and Downes (DD-375) took the brunt of the second wave of dive-bombing intended for USS Pennsylvania (BB-38). The torpedo-damaged cruiser Helena (CL-50) is on the right beyond the crane. Visible in the center distance are the capsized Oklahoma (BB-37) and Maryland (BB-46). This image was captured by Harold Fawcett. (NHHC, 80-G-19943.)

USS SHAW (DD-373) EXPLODES, DECEMBER 7, 1941. The forward magazine of USS *Shaw* (DD-373) exploded during the second Japanese attack wave. To the left of the explosion, *Shaw*'s stern is visible at the end of floating drydock YFD-2. At right is the bow of USS *Nevada* (BB-36), with a tug alongside fighting fires. The blast was photographed from Ford Island, with a dredging line in the foreground. (NHHC, 80-G-16871.)

RESCUING *WEST VIRGINIA* SURVIVORS, DECEMBER 7, 1941. The scale of the damage and the danger of cutting into fuel or munitions made rescue operations slow and difficult. Tapping could be heard on the hull of *West Virginia* (BB-48) for weeks, but the survivors could not be reached. A calendar marked for 16 days was found when the compartment was finally opened, too late to save anyone. (NHHC, 80-G-19930.)

WHEELER FIELD, DECEMBER 7, 1941. Wheeler Field was one of the chief targets of the attack. Eighty-three of the 90 aircraft were destroyed, a calculated first move the Japanese had made to prevent American aviators from being able to respond. Pictured is smoke rising from Wheeler Field directly following the attack. (NHHC, 50473.)

DESTROYED HANGAR, c. DECEMBER 7–10, 1941. The Japanese knew that crippling US planes as fast as possible meant that they would only have to evade return fire from the ground. Ships that could not move struggled to take down aircraft, even when they saw them coming. As Admiral Yarnell had demonstrated in 1932, aviation had indeed evolved to the point where battleships would no longer decide the outcome of wars. (USAMH, 4784.)

JAPANESE PLANE SHOT DOWN DURING PEARL HARBOR ATTACK, C. 1941. A Nakajima B5N-2 "Kate" from the Japanese aircraft carrier *Kaga* is being lifted by crane. The aircraft was shot down during the Japanese attack. (NHHC, 80-G-32684.)

JAPANESE MIDGET SUBMARINE GROUNDED DURING THE ATTACK, C. 1941. A beach patrol at Bellows Field discovered a damaged Japanese midget submarine and captured the first US prisoner of war. The submarine, *HA. 19*, had been depth-charged and struck a reef trying to escape. It drifted until it got lodged in the coral. The commanding officer, Kazuo Sakamaki, was taken prisoner, and "Japan's Secret Weapon" was paraded around as a reminder of the attack, helping to sell war bonds. (NHHC, 80-G-17016.)

USS ARIZONA (BB-39), 1916. No ship is more inexorably tied to December 7, 1941, than USS *Arizona* (BB-39). *Arizona* joined the Pacific Fleet in 1921. She was regularly deployed for training exercises and supported relief efforts after a 1933 California earthquake. The photograph shows *Arizona* returning to New York City in 1916 after sea trials. The "cage" or "Christmas tree" design of her masts was changed during her 1929 modernization. (Library of Congress.)

USS ARIZONA (BB-39) BURNING, DECEMBER 1941. Onboard USS *Arizona* (BB-39), air raid sirens went off at 7:55 a.m. Ten minutes later, her forward deck was struck by a 1,760-pound bomb that hit the ammunition magazine, triggering a massive explosion. The 33,000-ton vessel was lifted out of the water and torn in half. *Arizona* was still burning three days later on December 10. A total of 1,177 of the 1,512 crewmen on board were killed. (NHHC, NH 63918.)

FUNERAL AT NAVAL AIR STATION KANEOHE BAY, DECEMBER 8, 1941. Marine rifles fired a volley over the bodies of 15 officers and men killed at Naval Air Station Kaneohe Bay during the Pearl Harbor attack. These burial ceremonies took place on December 8, 1941. Note the sandbagged emplacement atop the small hill in the right middle distance. Even while mourning the dead, men were preparing for a possible second wave. (NHHC, 80-G-32854.)

FIRST PEARL HARBOR MEMORIAL SERVICE, 1942. At a joint memorial service held for men lost in USS *Arizona* (BB-39), USS *Utah* (BB-31), and USS *Oklahoma* (BB-37), Navy yard workers and sailors gathered with flowers sent by the families and friends of those who were lost. This 1942 ceremony was the first annual commemoration of the attack, but it would not be the last. USS *Arizona*, covered by a monument in 1962, is today still visited by millions from around the world. (HSA, PPFUR-1-21-006.)

DORIS MILLER RECEIVES THE NAVY CROSS FROM ADMIRAL NIMITZ, MAY 27, 1942. Doris Miller, steward's mate first class, was collecting laundry at 7:57 a.m. when torpedoes struck USS *West Virginia* (BB-38). Miller took control of a .50-caliber anti-aircraft gun and successfully shot down several Japanese planes. An officer then spotted Miller, who cut an imposing figure at six feet, three inches, and called for his help. The ship's captain, Mervyn Bennion, was wounded and needed to be moved to a safer location. After assisting his captain, Miller continued rescuing wounded men, saving many lives. In this photograph, Admiral Nimitz pins the Navy Cross on Doris Miller, the first Black American to receive this medal. Admiral Nimitz was elevated over 28 senior officers to command the Pacific Fleet. He took command aboard the submarine USS *Grayling* (SS-209). *Grayling* was lost with all hands off Manila some time around September 9, 1943. (Right, NHHC, 62656; below, NHHC, 62023.)

USS ARIZONA (BB-39) AFTER REMOVAL OF GUNS AND SLIDES. SEPTEMBER 23, 1943. This photograph shows the dangerous conditions of work salvaging ships damaged in the attack. The damage was so tremendous that salvage efforts continued for years while the war was being fought across the Pacific. (HSA, PPFUR-2-14-003.)

DAMAGED HOME OF PAUL GOO AT LILIHA AND KUAKINI STREETS. Goo's home was damaged and 84 civilians were killed or wounded during the December 7, 1941, attack. One family, the Hirasakis, took shelter at their saimin shop. Their eight-year-old son had run home after a shell struck his school. Another errant shell struck the restaurant, killing seven patrons, Joseph Jitsuo "Joe" Hirasaki, and his three children. Only their mother survived. (HWRD, 144.)

"THREE CIVILIANS DEAD," DECEMBER 7, 1941. This photograph, widely reproduced in the aftermath of the attack, carried the following somber caption: "Eight miles from the nearest military target—3 civilians dead." Many civilians who received damages got no reimbursement through insurance. Some kept bombed cars as souvenirs, refusing to be paid for them. (USAMH, 4762.)

DAMAGE AT McCULLY AND KING STREETS, DECEMBER 7, 1941.
A fire destroyed this building at McCully and King Streets in the heart of Mo'ili'ili, a historically Japanese neighborhood. What the public did not know was that almost all of the damage to civilian areas was caused not by Japanese planes but by the US military attempting to shoot them down. (HWRD, 152.)

"Where Projectiles Fell on Blitz Day," the *Honolulu Advertiser*. Police were very busy all day. Residents did not know what was happening, and some thought a military drill had gotten out of control. Bombs fell on schools, businesses, homes, and cars, downing power lines, starting fires, and killing civilians. An antiaircraft shell struck the auditorium of the first Japanese language school on Oahu while children were gathered there for a special assembly. Even after the attack ended, frantic civilians called the police constantly. Some reports proved to be completely unfounded (Japanese parachuting onto the beach), and other times officers arrived on the scene to discover that people had misunderstood what they saw. Police arrived at one address to apprehend looters, only to discover that they were removing valuables from their own home. An unexploded bomb was sitting in the living room. (PFSM.)

Dr. Howard O. Smith Jr. Caring for Patients aboard USS Solace (AH-5), December 1941. Doctors operated on the wounded as quickly as possible, passing surgical instruments from table to table and exhausting 2,000 units of plasma in six hours. Most anesthesia on the island was locked up and could not be obtained. (Navy Bureau of Medicine and Surgery Archives, 09-5043-31.)

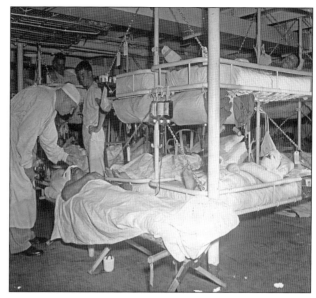

Local Women Assisting with Salvage Operations, c. 1942. Over the days that followed, civilians immediately rose to the challenges presented. All available manpower was directed to rescue and salvage efforts at Pearl Harbor. Police did not have enough guns for volunteers, so men with sugar cane knives and clubs patrolled the streets. Girl Scouts babysat hundreds of evacuated children, and Boy Scouts on bicycles passed information and directed traffic. (USAMH, 158.)

JAPANESE AMERICAN GRADUATES OF FARRINGTON HIGH SCHOOL, 1943. These Japanese American graduates took a final picture together before leaving for service in the US Army. From left to right are (first row) Alfred Arakaki, Robert Hashimoto, Stanley Hashimoto, James Horinouchi, Walter Ishiki, and Gary Ishimura; (second row) Masami Ito, Robert Katayama, Charles Kubota, Tsuneshi Maruo, Tsutomu Matsuno, Masaru Taira, Thomas Tamai and Fred Tani; (third row) Isamo Tsuchimoto, Masao Yamasaki, Harry Moromisata, and Hidenori Oganeku. (HWRD, 124.)

HONOULIULI INTERNMENT CAMP, C. 1944. On the mainland, Japanese Americans were forced away from coastal areas to internment camps. Hawaii's government vehemently opposed this plan. Many people of Japanese ancestry were civic leaders and essential workers. Four hundred civilians were still sent to Honouliuli Internment on Oahu. The camp was also used to house 4,000 prisoners of war. Internees called it "Jigoku-Dani" (Hell Valley) due to the heat. (Courtesy of the Japanese Cultural Center of Hawaii.)

DANIEL K. INOUYE, 1945. Born in Honolulu to immigrant parents, Daniel K. Inouye joined the US Army as soon as it dropped its ban on Japanese Americans. His unit, the 442nd, adopted the motto "Go for broke" (Hawaiian pidgin for "Give 100 percent"). Twenty-one members received medals of honor, including Inouye. Recovering at Percy Jones Army Hospital after losing his arm, Inouye befriended another young officer, Bob Dole. Both men became US senators. (Robert and Elizabeth Dole Archive and Special Collections.)

FRANCIS WAI, c. 1943. About 2,000 Hawaiians or part-Hawaiians served in the US Army during World War II. One of them, Capt. Francis B. Wai, received the Distinguished Service Cross posthumously for valor during the invasion of Leyte with the 24th Infantry Division. A graduate of Punahou School, Wai enlisted in the Hawaii National Guard and was called to active duty in 1940. He was killed in action on October 20, 1944. (National Museum of the US Army.)

WOMEN IN THE NAVY, 1945. WAVES (Women Accepted for Volunteer Emergency Service) was a branch of the Naval Reserve, created so that women could fill essential noncombat roles. It was not until nearly the end of the war that WAVES were sent to Hawaii. Pictured are Storekeeper 2nd Class Francella Leigh, Yeoman 2nd Class Patricia McRae, and Pharmacist's Mate 3rd Class Suzanne Hosmer in their stateroom en route to their new duty stations at Pearl Harbor in January 1945. (NHHC 80-G-47597.)

EN ROUTE TO PEARL HARBOR, 1945. On board USS *General Omar Bundy* (AP-152), WAVES enjoy a little sun in June 1945. Approximately 100,000 women served in the WAVES during World War II. (NHHC 80-G-330782.)

CHILI WILLIAMS, 1945. Morale was boosted by USO performers who flew across the Pacific providing entertainment for servicemen. USS *Bowfin* (SS-287) crewmember Walter Beyer captured this shot of famous pinup girl Chili Williams, the "polka dot girl." After a photograph of her wearing a polka-dot bikini appeared in an issue of *LIFE* magazine, Williams received over 100,000 fan letters. (PFSM, 2015.0001.013BG.)

KAMEHAMEHA I STATUE BY GEORGE BACON, C. 1945. The story goes that it was suggested at the outbreak of World War II to remove the famous Kamehameha statue across from Iolani Palace in order to protect it. Locals refused. The sentiment was that Kamehameha would not have retreated and, therefore, neither would Hawaii. (HSA, PPBAC-2-14-012.)

WAR SAVINGS STAMPS POSTER, C. 1944. Hawaii's unique blend of cultures is evidenced by this poster advertising War Savings Stamps in English, Hawaiian, Tagalog, Portuguese, Korean, Chinese, and Japanese. Despite being under martial law for the entirety of World War II, Hawaii did not become a US state until 1959. (PFSM, 2001.0001.004.)

USS Arizona (BB-39), the Ship Whose Loss Started World War II. The remains of USS *Arizona* (BB-39) at Pearl Harbor are guarded today by USS *Missouri* (BB-63), the battleship upon whose deck the Japanese surrender was signed. This photograph was taken in 2024 from the deck of the submarine USS *Bowfin* (SS-287). Few who remember World War II are still alive, but the descendants of those who served still make pilgrimages to Pearl Harbor. Much of what the US military built on Oahu for World War II is now crumbling. The prospect of war today does not look like it did in 1941. Missiles are fired from thousands of miles away. Satellites serve as lookouts. Many would like to see a reduction of the military presence in Hawaii, but in an increasingly tense world, Pearl Harbor will likely always remain an essential foothold for the United States in the Pacific. (Author's photograph.)

Discover Thousands of Local History Books Featuring Millions of Vintage Images

Arcadia Publishing, the leading local history publisher in the United States, is committed to making history accessible and meaningful through publishing books that celebrate and preserve the heritage of America's people and places.

Find more books like this at
www.arcadiapublishing.com

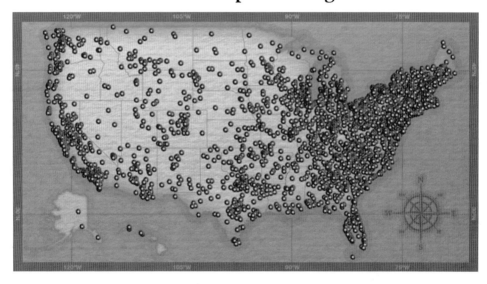

Search for your hometown history, your old stomping grounds, and even your favorite sports team.